REASON WOUNDED

Reason Wounded

An Experience of India's Emergency

PRIMILA LEWIS

London
GEORGE ALLEN & UNWIN
Boston   Sydney

First published in India in 1978
First published in Great Britain in 1979

GEORGE ALLEN & UNWIN LTD
40 Museum Street, London WC 1A 1LU

© Primila Lewis, 1978, 1979

ISBN 0-04 301096 2

Printed in India

Preface

This book is based on the journals I kept while in jail for eighteen months during the emergency. It was written during a period of three months in Oxford, England, where I joined my husband and son after my release from prison.

My detention under MISA was the culmination of a series of events in the course of a struggle for the minimum legal and human rights of agricultural workers employed on the VIP farms of the Mehrauli *tehsil* on the southern outskirts of Delhi. This struggle of the impoverished, immigrant *purabias* for minimum wages, minimum job security, and basic democratic rights was waged against some of the outstanding political, military, industrial and social figures of India.

The response of this elite to the stirrings of democratic consciousness in their workers was a revelation of the truly feudal authoritarianism of the most educated and priviledged of our upper classes. What was even more revealing was that the entire might of the administrative and police forces of the capital city— notwithstanding the protestations of a few individuals within these—was ranged behind the VIPs, irrespective of the fact that they were violating practically every law in the book.

It was brought home to all of us, optimistic about our right to struggle for the implementation of various progressive laws passed by the socialist government of Mrs Gandhi, that when the poor man raises his voice for justice, he will be clubbed down unceremoniously. And anyone who protests, resists or refuses to be cowed down will be dubbed 'subversive' or 'extremist', and hounded, harassed, and repressed.

It is a hard fact, that until democracy is extended beyond the right to vote—to the right to work, to eat, to live decently and with dignity—our democracy is for the birds and our progressives are mere paper tigers.

All of us who want to prevent dictatorship must extend our democratic consciousness beyond ourselves to the impoverished toilers of our country, without whom we cannot exist, let alone build a society of honour rather than shame. This, in essence, is the truth I have learned, both inside and outside prison. I hope I have been able to communicate it as a concrete experience in this book.

I would like to thank some of the friends whose criticisms and suggestions at various stages in the writing helped me greatly. My husband Charles, with his patience and discretion, was a constant support. Shyam Bhatia, Peter Lewis, Urvashi Butalia, Nanu and Bill Mitchell, and Rajiv Kumar, rendered valuable editorial and critical help. To all these, and a few others like Patty and Stephan, my grateful thanks. Also to Govind Swaminadhan for his generous legal advice.

But it remains to be noted that this book would never have been written were it not for all those whom I cannot name here: all those struggling for dignity and justice, and from whom I learned about reality and life.

PRIMILA LEWIS

Contents

Part One	*3*
Part Two	*29*
Part Three	*101*
Part Four	*177*
Appendix	*185*
Glossary	*197*
Abbreviations	*201*
Index	*203*

Prologue

"In the words of the great Christian divine Dean Farrer, 'there are two mighty and noble feelings which may sway the human heart, one, the pity for individual suffering, the pity which, like the new-born babe, sits in the heart of a John Howard or a Vincent de Paul, the other, the passionate indignation for human wrongs. There are souls which feel wounded when reason is wounded; which, moved by a masculine sensibility, are keenly alive to the mighty interests of order, justice and human dignity. The spirit of man plunged in ignorance and error, liberty of person fettered, liberty of conscience strangled, justice perverted, innocence oppressed, reason hurled down by violence, multitudes crushed by a selfish despotism—these are the wrongs which fill their souls with flames. And what are these but violations of the Christian law, "Do unto others as ye would they should do unto you," violations of that holy law on a vaster scale, and transferred from the individual to the social sphere.'

'Darkly and terribly guilty are they,' says the same divine, 'who are living in wilful and constant violation of God; all they —every one of them—who sell themselves to do evil, who *work all* uncleanliness with greediness; who call evil good and good evil, who are gaining their livelihoods in ways which demoralize or degrade or defraud their neighbours. *Guilty* also are all those —and they are many—who without active and flagrant immorality, live only to the world or to the flesh; selfish, egotistical, indifferent, caring only for their own comfort or interest, shut up amid their own refinements and indulgences, heedless of the blowing winds which wrestle on the great deep without, and of multitudes who are being helplessly swallowed up in those wild waves. *Less guilty*, yet still needing to be aroused to nobler aims, are the multitudes who, though not useless, not immoral, yet too blind to the solemn responsibilities which God lays upon us all, raise no finger outside the circle of their own narrow domesticities to make the world happier or better.

Least guilty, yet not wholly to be acquitted, are those who do love and pity their suffering fellowmen, but, folding their hands in mute despair before the perplexities of life's awful problems, need to be fired with fresh energies and brighter hopes'."

Quoted by Lala Lajpat Rai,
in *Mission of the Arya Samaj*, 1912.

1

"Thoreau has said, 'In the reign of a government which impri-
sons its people unjustly, the place of every self-respecting man
is in jail'!"

Laxman Tripathi in *Barrack Chayya*

THE AIR INDIA FLIGHT REACHED PALAM AIRPORT, NEW Delhi around 7 o'clock of the morning of 2 July, 1975. Karoki, our eight year old son, and I had left my husband Charles at Heathrow the day before, full of foreboding after the declaration of the state of emergency by Mrs Gandhi on 26 June. But Karoki was due to go to boarding school in Chandigarh and there had been no last minute messages from India advising us not to come. I knew that I had antagonised some of the most powerful people in the country, including Mrs Gandhi herself, as a result of the agricultural workers union I had organised and the agitation we had launched on their farms in the southern outskirts of the city of Delhi. But I had not been involved in the opposition movement led by Jayaprakash Narayan which had been made the immediate excuse for clamping the emergency on the country. My own work had been entirely lawful, and apart for reasons of malice, there were no grounds whatsoever for the government to take action against me. But malice was by no means to be discounted, and it was with some apprehension that I watched the plane taxi to a halt from the window near my seat.

Karoki and I were among the first out. We passed through Health, and I caught a glimpse of friends waiting to meet us in the glass-enclosed lounge above. But there was no sign of Srilata and my heart sank. She was my co-worker in the union and I had been expecting her to meet me.

At Immigration, the officer looked at my passport, then at

me, and said with an interested gleam in his eye, "Mrs Primila
Lewis?" He whispered to another officer by his side who went
off and whispered to somebody else, while the passengers
behind us swept past and on to Customs.

So it's on, I thought. My apprehensions seemed to be confirmed, but I tried to push such thoughts from my mind. Nothing
had been said as yet; it might be some mistake. There was no
point in jumping to conclusions.

We waited for a long time. Upstairs, my friends must have
been wondering what was happening. I kept asking what the
matter was, only getting, "In a few minutes. Please wait," very
politely but firmly in reply. Karoki was very tired, he had
hardly slept all night and was restless now, wanting to know
why we were being held up. Eventually I was told I could take
my baggage into Customs. Again there was much whispering
between the Immigration and Customs men, and I was getting
increasingly alarmed and mystified by all the secrecy. My
friends upstairs, who I could see clearly now, looked grave but
tried to cheer me with a thumbs-up sign. Again it was a long
wait. The passengers off our flight had just about gone and
those from new arrivals were coming in. At last, after about an
hour and a half, a Customs officer motioned me forward and
went perfunctorily through our things.

There was no point in making for the exit as the hall had
quietly filled up with police. I was told that I must go to the
International Departure Lounge and wait there till there were
further instructions.

"For God's sake why?" I burst out. "My friends have been
waiting so long—at least tell them what is happening and
how long it will take, if you can't tell me. And can't my son go
to them? He's only a child."

They were very polite, but ushered us both into the International Departure Lounge saying that they would send word to
my friends, I was not to worry, it would only take a few more
minutes now.

An hour passed and nothing happened. Then an Air India
official came in and asked if I was Mrs Lewis.

"Your friends are waiting outside. They have sent me in to
find out how long you'll be," he said.

"I wish I knew," I told him. "They've just made us sit here

and I simply don't know why or for how long."

"Are they going to deport you?" he asked.

"I don't see why," I replied.

Then a policeman came up and whispered something to the official who slipped away without another word. I wondered if he would be able to say anything to my friends, or if they were still as much in the dark as I was. I didn't know whether to ask them to stay or go and was not even sure that any message I sent them would be delivered. Karoki was getting more and more restless and a little scared and bewildered, asking again and again, "But why can't we go, Mama? What are they going to do?"

I was too filled with helplessness and dread to be able to comfort him, and could only say, "I don't know little boy. We must just wait and see. They will tell us soon. Play with your cars, darling—or try to sleep—you are so tired."

But he shook his head.

"I can't sleep, Mama. When can we go?"

I didn't know. It's an 'emergency', I thought. No laws apply any more. Only the will of the people on top and the whims of their stooges below. There was no point in asking questions or making protests and demands. 'Legal rights' did not exist in an 'emergency' and we were at the mercy of the powers above.

The lounge in which we sat and waited was empty except for the policemen who were unobtrusively hanging around but were obviously there for me. At one point a shopkeeper from one of the duty-free shops sidled up and asked me to follow him into his shop where he would tell me what all this was about. Was my husband an American? he asked meaningfully, and wanted to know what passport I had. He was quite off the track I was sure, although my husband was a foreigner, English not American, and my passport was Indian. The police had also said something about my passport not being right, but I was sure it was only a ploy to sidetrack my questions.

At about 12.30 p.m., an armed posse of seven or eight policemen led by a burly Sikh officer entered the lounge and marched briskly up to us. I felt Karoki's alarm.

"Mrs Lewis? I am the Station House Officer, Parliament Street police station. You are to come with me please."

"But what is happening? Why?" I asked, as we were escorted

out and into a waiting taxi. "Please let me send this child to my friends at least. . . ."

"I'm sorry Madam, I have orders to take you both to the Parliament Street police station. The District Magistrate and the DSP sahib are waiting for you there and they will answer all your questions. We will tell your friends to follow you there."

The Station House Officer (SHO) and two policewomen who were waiting in the taxi accompanied Karoki and me and we drove off. It was strange to see the familiar streets, houses and people of the city. I was no longer a free agent.

Parliament Street. We reached the police station with the judicial courts on its right. The people hanging about the corridors outside the court rooms were a familiar sight. Those courts had been the scene of so many fruitless, wasted, unjust events. We were taken into the office of the Deputy Superintendent of Police (DSP). He was a youngish man, quiet mannered and polite. There was no sign of the District Magistrate.

The DSP asked us to sit down.

"Mrs Lewis," he said, "I am ordered to arrest you under the Maintenance of Internal Security Act. The Daryaganj police will be here shortly to take custody of you. If there is anything you need or anyone you wish to contact please do it now. When you leave this place I cannot guarantee what will happen."

So it was MISA after all. I was being held under the notorious preventive detention law that had only recently been made more stringent with the excuse that it was going to be used against economic offenders such as black marketeers and smugglers. But Mrs Gandhi had used it to put all her opponents behind bars instead, since the declaration of the emergency a week ago.

Karoki began to cry as I told him in a whisper what this meant. I held him close to me and told him not to worry; this was something which could have happened at any time because the government didn't like those who worked for the poor. But it wouldn't be for long, I was sure, and I would soon be with him again.

"I want my Daddy," he cried. "Please Mama, I want to go back to Daddy."

"Yes, darling, I promise. I'll ring the office just now and they will put you on the first plane back. Don't you worry little boy, you'll be with him very soon."

I held him close to me. Poor little boy. The DSP looked away and the burly SHO leaned over to me and whispered, "Don't cry, Madam, he'll only feel it worse."

"Yes, yes I know. That's why I'm—"

I met the DSP's eyes. He looked pained.

"Mrs Lewis, I'm only acting under orders."

"I know, I know. Are you going to arrest him too?"

"Of course not! Can somebody take custody of him?"

"My friends were at the airport but I don't know if they were told to come here. May I use your telephone?"

"Of course, please go ahead," he pushed his telephone towards me.

I rang my husband's office. The operator greeted me warmly.

"You're back! How are you? How is Mr Lewis? When will he come back?"

"I'm fine, thanks, Charles is too. He will be back in October. May I speak to Mr Dayal please?" She put me on to him.

"Ravi? This is Primila. Look, I'm at the Parliament Street police station. Can you come here?"

"I'll come right away," he said, sounding as if he knew what had happened. It was quite possible of course, especially if Srilata had been arrested earlier, that he expected there would be trouble for me as well.

When he came, calm as usual, but serious, he confirmed my fears about Srilata. When I told him that Karoki wanted to go back to England he very sensibly suggested that we wait a day or two to let him calm down and then decide. We agreed that Karoki should be sent to my parents in Chandigarh where he was also due to go to school. He assured me that they would do whatever Karoki himself wanted after he had thought things over. The DSP told him that Karoki would have to go with me to the Daryaganj police station and he could take him over only after that. Meanwhile if I needed anything in the way of clothes, soap, towels or cigarettes etc., he could get these for me now.

I did need all these things, having only warm clothes with me in my suitcase, all of which, except for a pair of cotton pants and a *lungi*, were inappropriate for the Indian summer. But clothes and sandals would have to wait; right now Ravi could buy me some soap, a towel, and cigarettes, and he went off to get these.

I wanted to change into cooler things now, and the men left the room to allow me some privacy. As I was bending over my suitcase, the door burst open and one of the friends who had been waiting at the airport rushed in. So they had told her where I was going. We embraced each other and she told me that her husband, who had also been at the airport, had had to go to work since it had got so late. I asked her about Srilata. She told me they had picked her up from her flat on the 26th of June, the day the emergency had been declared.

"God, I hope I'll be put with her," I said.

"I bet you won't be." She was bitter. "But don't you worry about Karoki, we'll take very good care of him."

I changed my clothes and then, when the Daryaganj police turned up, Karoki and I set off for the police station, and my friend who had to meet Ravi in the office to get a few things sorted out said they would both come back for Karoki later.

He was in complete control of himself by now but very quiet. When my friends returned to take him away, he slid off my lap and smiled shyly at me.

"Bye, Mama," he said.

After that it was a long, long wait. The police officers insisted I share their lunch which they were having late, no doubt because of me. A plump Muslim woman, attractive and trying hard to please, perhaps because she was in some kind of trouble, had cooked a special meat curry for the DSP and SHO. She had ordered *rumali rotis*, a Moghul speciality of very thin unleavened bread, cold mangoes, and iced water which was very welcome in the sweltering heat. But I wasn't hungry. The policewoman by my side put an arm around me.

"It's because of her little boy; he was with her," she said sympathetically. I shook my head and feeling a complete fool, burst into tears. If only they would't mention Karoki, I thought, knowing that was the one thing which would break my control just now.

At 5 p.m., the District Majistrate's written order for my detention "under the powers conferred by sub-section 3(1) of
Section 16-A of the Maintenance of Internal Security Act, 1971"
was delivered by a despatch rider. So this was what we had
been waiting for. But there was yet another wait before transport and a guard were available, and then at last I was driven
off in a police jeep to the Tihar Central Jail.

On the way we were held up at a railway crossing. There had
been an accident. A man had been run over by a train and
there was no way of getting through. While we waited, the
driver of the jeep, a great hulk of a man, asked me why I had
been arrested.

"I don't know," I told him. "I was working in a union of
agricultural workers in Mehrauli where all these bigwigs have
their farms and they didn't like what I was doing, I suppose."

The policewoman said, "Her little boy was with her when
she was arrested. She is feeling very bad."

"*Behnchod!*"* the driver cursed. "They are doing wrong. That
woman is going too far." He was referring to Mrs Gandhi.

The road ahead cleared up after a while and we crossed the
railway line and soon reached the great iron gates of the
prison. A small door cut into the gate was opened and we
stepped into a large hall on either side of which were offices. I
was taken into one of these by a young Sikh officer who
searched my things and took away the needles, scissors, pens,
and money I had with me, saying that none of these was
allowed inside.

"Is Miss Swaminadhan here?" I asked anxiously.

"Yes, she's here."

"I want to be put with her please," I said.

"Yes, you will be with her," was the reply.

I didn't know what to expect. This was my first experience
of prison and I was nervous. The matron was called. She was a
huge, hawk-faced woman dressed in a khaki *salwar-kameez*. She
looked like a camp commander from Belsen.

"Don't worry, everything will be all right," she said gently,
putting an arm around me.

She led me out of the lobby through another large iron gate

*"Sister-fucker!"

and into a big grassy yard with trees and high-walled compounds all round. I was taken into one of these compounds—the female ward or *Zenana Khana*.

A group of women were sitting under a tree playing cards.

"Srilata!"

She looked up without recognition, then went on playing.

"*Sri!*"

She looked up again, then leapt to her feet and ran to me. We clung to one another.

"Oh my God, its you!" she cried. "I've been waiting and looking out all day and then I gave up, thinking you wouldn't come. You look different," she leaned back to look at me, "like your old photographs!" We laughed. I had put on ten pounds in England and my hair was cut short.

The women were excited. Srilata's friend had come at last! They crowded round and Sri introduced me to them. Then she showed me our lodging. It was a small room, actually a converted office, which we would share. There were no bars on the doors and windows, a fair-sized verandah in front and a couple of small trees just beyond. Srilata ordered everybody out and then we sat down on her cot and talked.

I caught up on all the news and on the developments in the Union during my absence of five weeks in England. I was relieved to find Srilata relaxed and cheerful. She told me how the police had knocked at her door before dawn on 26 June, and how she had been driven away to the police station where, to her relief, she had found hundreds of other people who had also been arrested, including Mrs Gandhi's arch opponent Raj Narain, who had instituted legal proceedings against her for election malpractices, a charge which the Allahabad High Court had recently upheld and which, indeed, had been one of the reasons for imposing the emergency.

But later, as I watched Sri, I saw that she was not as relaxed as she at first appeared. She did not eat and at night she could not sleep. She told me it had been like this since her arrest. I had a healthy appetite myself, and as for sleep, after the flight, the tensions of the day and the late hours talking with Srilata, I dropped off and slept like a log all night.

The next day Sri told me why she was so tense.

"I keep having visions of interrogations and torture, Primila," she said. "Every time that door into the ward rattles and a warder comes in I think, that's it—they've come for me!"

I did not think it likely that we would be tortured. They had treated us quite well till now. But I understood her fears. There had been so many reports in the press about the misuse of black laws like MISA and the inhuman torture of people in detention without trial for long years. We were cut off from communication or help and from the normal course of the law as well. Anything could in fact happen. But we decided to be sensible and cross our hurdles as they came. In the meantime we would keep ourselves fit and cheerful by organising a regular daily routine of activity which would include study, exercise and a systematic attempt to get to know our fellow inmates.

Sri showed me the ropes. Where to bathe (under the borewell tap, in cold, splashing water under the brilliant sun) and where to go for 'nature's calls' (the open drain behind our room after dark), the only lavatories being for the use of the criminal prisoners and filthy beyond belief. We did the rounds of the barracks and cells visiting all the inmates, most of whom were under trial for various offences. They were an amazing assortment: young and old, quiet and vulgar, shy and fierce—a boisterous, quarrelsome, friendly lot. Among them was the attractive Chandresh Sharma who had hit the headlines some months ago in a high-society murder case, and, high on a trip, a drugged Brazilian girl who just sat and stared with a strange smile on her face.

Even the most aggressive and obscene-mouthed of the women seemed intensely human. Longing to show, to give and to receive affection and friendship, ready to whip round and tear your eyes out if you angered them, but otherwise only too ready to please. They fed us all day with rounds of tea and snacks made on their makeshift stoves. This was against the rules, but everything goes in jail, one soon learns, if you can keep the warders 'happy'.

Although we wanted to do our own work, clean out our room, fill our water containers from the borewell which was the only source of water in the ward, wash our own clothes, etc., the younger girls who had already become very attached to Srilata simply would not hear of it and insisted on doing everything for us. We saw we would have to tread a careful course between not offending them and yet making them understand that we did not believe in a master-servant relationship but wanted to establish real friendship with them.

The prison welfare officer came to see us in the evening and gave us a postcard each to send to our parents. We were able to inform them that we were well, unharmed and in perfectly tolerable surroundings. We also decided to send a letter to the Delhi Administration, the body directly responsible for our detention, challenging our arrest. Our morale was high and we were confident that we would see this detention through to-gether with ease and even profit to ourselves and that it wouldn't last very long anyway.

So passed the 2nd and 3rd July. On the 4th, two days after my arrest, I received word to pack up my things and come to the office. A warder escorted me out, holding an umbrella over my head to protect me from the sun, and on my asking him what it was all about said vaguely, "Maybe they are going to release you." I went back slowly to Sri, standing behind the barred entrance to the ward.

"He says it may be a release," I told her with trepidation at the thought of leaving her alone.

She said, quickly, "God! It may be an interrogation—it could take days. Listen Primila, if you get out, come back between 8 and 9 p.m. and toot outside on the road, I'll hear you from here." We decided on a signal. She gave me some detective stories, Shaw's *St. Joan*, a cotton nightie, and stood there, one foot resting on the other, her beautiful dark eyes watching me sadly as I walked away.

Dear friend and even dearer work-mate! How much we had shared and battled through together. Her detention was even more unfair and illogical than mine. She had become active in the Union only recently and had been concentrating more on the legal aspects of the work than on the agitation on the farms.

I was taken to the Jail Superintendent's office. Sitting with him was a Sub-Divisional Magistrate (SDM).

"What is happening." I asked. "Can I be told?"

They wouldn't say, but they watched me thoughtfully and said that they were waiting for the DSP to arrive. This refusal to answer questions, to explain what was happening, was mystifying and created tension. One felt like an object being shunted about 'by order' by officials who were oblivious to the fact that one was a person and not a thing. They were not unkind so much as terrified of showing any sympathy and reacting like human beings. Typical bureaucrats, it was too much to expect any more of them.

Three men came into the room. They were obviously politicians under detention too and looked important. They wanted to know what was up. Were we being transferred? I envied their brisk self-confidence as a Superintendent glanced nervously at the SDM who shrugged. The Superintendent nodded. Where to? He did not know; they were waiting for the DSP who should have been here by now.

The officials were anxious. It seemed that lorry-loads of more detenues were expected to arrive any moment and they wanted us out of the way before that because if we met there could have been trouble. At last the DSP bustled in. Who should it be but old Mokhum Singh! We had had many a tangle with Mokhum Singh when he had been the SHO at the Mehrauli Police Station. So he had been promoted to the rank of DSP. How typical. We had been assured by his superiors that he had been suspended because of his malafide activities while in charge of 'law and order' in the Mehrauli district. We took each other in without recognition or salute.

Twenty of us were being transferred somewhere else. A police guard armed with submachine-guns lined up on either side of the van parked outside the jail gate and we climbed in. As we drove off the detenues shouted slogans:

"*Indira Teri Tanashahi—Nahi Chalegi, Nahi Chalegi!*" ("Indira your dictatorship won't last!")

"*Lok Nayak Jayaprakash—Zindabad! Zindabad!*" (Long live the popular leader Jayaprakash!")

"*Har Zor Zulum Ke Takkar Me—Sangharsh Hamara Nara Hai!*" ("In every struggle against repression, resistance is our cry!")

Then everyone slumped back and took stock of one another.

"You are a labour leader aren't you?" a plump, spectacled

man said to me. "Why have they arrested you?"

"I don't know."

"Are you CPI(M)?"

"No, no party, but our union recently affiliated with AITUC, the CPI union."

"CPI (M)?"

"No, it's the CPI," I said with a smile.

"That's odd!"

Odd indeed, I agreed with him mentally. The two parliamentary, communist parties, the Communist Party of India (CPI) and the Communist Party of India (Marxist) (CPI-M) had taken contrary positions towards Mrs Gandhi. The CPI, who saw her as leading the 'progressive' sections of the Congress Party had given her their full support and were loud in their acclamation of the emergency now, which they saw as a move against the right. But the CPI (M) regarded Mrs Gandhi and her ruling party as a whole as 'reactionary' and had given passive support to the opposition movement against her, thus earning her wrath against them too, when she cracked down on the country on 26 June.

The detenus introduced themselves to me. They were mostly from the Jan Sangh (People's Union) Party, the strongest and best organised party of the right wing besides the Congress, and among them was the ex-mayor of Delhi, Vijay Kumar Malhotra, and the President of the Delhi University Students' Union, Arun Jaitly. There were several white-bearded old gentlemen from the Jamaat-e-Islami and the Muslim Majlis, two Muslim organisations held to be communal. Apart from these, there were two members of the Socialist Party, a few RSS men (the RSS or Rashtriya Svayam Sevak Sangh—National Volunteer Service Corps—was a communal organisation on the extreme right and the ideological and organisational springboard of the Jan Sangh), and two others. One of these latter, a small, unshaven, plump young man announced, "And we are from the CPI(M-L)," with emphasis on the last syllables. The CPI (M-L) or Communist Party of India (Marxist-Leninist) is one of the Maoist or Naxalite groups of the revolutionary Left in India.

Everyone began to talk and exchange notes. When the young Naxalite spoke the whole van became silent.

"You all believe in this parliamentary system—we don't," he said. "But what were all of you doing, you who talk so loudly about democracy, when we Naxalites were being mercilessly killed and tortured a few years ago, and even now, when thousands have been rotting in jail without trial for years on end? I was arrested in Delhi in 1971 and tortured, then taken to Patna and tortured again, then to Calcutta—we were given electric shocks, heated, iron bars were stuffed up our backsides, young men have been maimed and driven mad—all these things are well known. But nobody, not one of you in your precious parliament raised a voice of protest or even of question!"

His voice shook with passion and no one said a word. The man sitting next to me, a gentle-faced Jan Sanghi, said, "This will be at least three months."

"For us it will be longer," the Naxalite said, shaking his head.

"No, no. The same rules will apply for everyone this time. Let us see if Parliament is convened. The Monsoon Session won't be of course, but they will have to convene it after six months otherwise Parliament itself is finished."

They all watched the road to try and make out where we were going. Down Mall Road, past Kingsway Camp, out of the city limits and on to the Chandigarh road. Would it be Rohtak? Hissar? Ambala? No one knew, but as each turn-off passed we knew that it would not be that one. Every time we passed a bazaar or crowded place the men shouted slogans. The Naxalites shouted "*Inquilab Zindabad!*" (Long Live Revolution) and everyone joined in lustily. The young Naxalite came over to me.

"I have heard about your work in Mehrauli. Are you a Marxist-Leninist?"

"I don't know enough about it yet," I answered. "What do you do?"

"Nothing now. I am inactive since several years."

So what did it mean? Your name on a list and you would be picked up every time, just for old times' sake? I felt sick. I wanted to join the men in their slogans but I could not articulate the words. The student leader came and sat next to me.

"They say we are RSS," he said. "You see that old man?" he pointed to a handsome, erect, white-haired old man sitting opposite us. "He is the north zone head of the RSS. This is the first time I have ever set eyes on him. They call us CIA stooges, but the communists are selling this country out to Russia. They call us reactionaries, but we want real socialism, only it should be a *national* socialism. We regard the Naxalites as the only genuine 'lefts' in this country."

Having delivered himself of this, he went off to sit by Vijay Kumar Malhotra, who sat quietly looking out of the widow throughout the journey. The kindly faced man on my right said, "You must join our party, the Jan Sangh. We want people like you, people who are delicated to the poor. You must contact us at our office when this is over."

"I have no faith in any of the political parties," I told him.

"Never mind. If we can win you, well and good, if not, at least we will have tried, and no harm will have been done." He smiled at me and I nodded and smiled back.

I noted with interest that all these men, drawn from such diverse political trends, had developed a comradely, good-humoured and considerate attitude to one another in their common adversity. They had shared some good days in the Tihar Jail in Delhi and they told me how each evening since their arrest they had gathered together and discussed their respective party stands and the general political situation in the country. It was a chance to get to know and understand one another in a way they had never done outside in the heat and conflict of parliamentary and electoral battles. How lucky they were to be together like this, I thought. Being a woman was such a disadvantage: one was almost invariably the only one, and alone in situations like these.

It grew dark. We were well on our way to Chandigarh. We stopped once for tea and once for a pee. The men were getting desperate for the latter and when the van would not stop to let them out, the old RSS leader threatened to pee straight out of the window.

"At my age I'm past caring," he laughed.

I was struck by his bold frankness and dignity. I had not expected this in an RSS man, assuming that they would all be extremely tradition-bound and feudal.

We passed the city of Karnal, then Ambala City and just beyond, at the great bend to the right for Chandigarh, we turned off left. "Ambala!" everyone chorused.

We were tired and cramped. The armed guard lined up outside the jail gates and we were let out of the van. Inside we were received by a tall, good-looking officer with huge handle-bar moustaches, and we had to wait while he searched our things. Then the men were taken in and I waited for the matron to come for me. She was fat, head draped in a white *dupatta* or veil, dark eyes lowered coyly, mouth a little open showing the gap between her front teeth. This was Swaran Kaur, I was told, and asked to follow her.

The female ward was close by, just next to the offices. I walked into a large open yard surrounded by high walls, with four or five single-storeyed brick buildings, two huge trees, and a few faces peering out from the barred window of one of the barracks. We went into a small room on the left of the entrance to the ward; it was very like the one in Tihar. A woman raised her head from the *charpai* or cot on which she had been asleep and blinked at us in the bright light. I was pleased to find there was another detenue here after all. She introduced herself as Dr Kamla Verma, member of the All-India Working Committee of the Jan Sangh, from Yamunanagar in Haryana, and she looked very disappointed on seeing me and realising that I was not one of her party comrades. Although it was late, well after midnight, I was given a meal, a bed was brought in for me, and after talking for a while, we slept.

Why had it all happened? Why this sudden declaration of emergency, these massive arrests, this suspension of the law, of the freedom of the press, of the judiciary and of all fundamental rights of the people?

Was it merely thirst for power that had made Mrs Gandhi declare a state of emergency in order to save herself from the Allahabad High Court judgement against her, on the charge of electoral malpractices, which would have disqualified her from holding or seeking office for six years?

Was it that the opposition movement led by Jayaprakash Narayan had assumed serious enough proportions to warrant an emergency being declared? Or did the reasons lie deeper? I thought of our work in Mehrauli and the implications of my own arrest for having attempted to give substance to the law—

for doing what the government and Mrs Gandhi above all had themselves clamoured about so loudly, and I began to think that it was a combination of several factors that had led up to the present drastic situation.

The movement led by Jayaprakash Narayan, veteran Gandhian and *Sarvodaya* leader, against the corruption, malfunctioning, and high-handedness of the Congress government headed by Mrs Gandhi, had certainly assumed countrywide proportions in the months before. Large sections of the middle classes, especially the students and youth, fed up with formal education and the futility of degrees which got them nowhere in the face of rising unemployment, spearheaded the movement. Housewives beating empty *thalis* or metal plates to signify their discontent with rising prices came into the streets, and children took out processions with placards reading "Give us bread not bullets." Begun in the cities, the movement began to spread into the villages as well, but developed primarily into a massive demonstration of middle class discontent.

In 1974 a similar massive and sustained but largely spontaneous movement, precipitated by the students in Gujarat, had brought down the corrupt and discredited Congress government of that state. Following the example of Gujarat, JP, as Jayaprakash Narayan is popularly known, took up the banner in Bihar. He was immediately joined by thousands of enthusiastic young men and women who fanned out through the state and urged the people to bring down the even more incompetent and corrupt Congress state government of Bihar. Slogans of 'Total Revolution', the right to recall discredited politicians, and 'Satyagraha', the Gandhian way of peaceful resistance, caught the imagination of the people all over the country and the movement soon spilled out of Bihar into other states as well. The more adamantly Mrs Gandhi and the government rejected the demand that the Bihar government step down, the more vociferous did the voice for its overthrow become.

JP's weakness, I think, lay in the fact that he had no organisation of his own with which to sustain the movement along the lines he envisaged. This, apart from the even more basic weakness that the lines of the 'Total Revolution' he envisaged were themselves vague and rather confused, gave various opposition parties and groups the opportunity of coming into the movement and trying to channel it in their own interests. The Right, headed by the Jan Sangh, lost no time in joining the movement and becoming an indispensable organisational factor in it.

The Socialist Party also joined the movement enthusiastically. The communist parties, arguing about theoretical issues and what class JP represented, took at least three different positions. The Moscow-aligned CPI rejected JP and his movement in toto, proclaiming it a CIA-backed plot of American imperialism to launch a fascist onslaught against Mrs Gandhi's 'progressive' government.

The other major Left parliamentary party, the CPI (M), took a halfway stand, supporting the democratic and 'anti-Congress' demands of the movement, but refusing to join it because of the presence of 'reactionary forces', particularly of the Jan Sangh, in it.

The non-parliamentary Left, comprising the communist revolutionaries, the Naxalites or Maoists as they are called, was also divided on this issue. Some of them, notably the CPI (M-L) faction led by Satya Narain Singh of Bihar, hailed the movement as a great democratic offensive against the fascist regime of Indira Gandhi, and joined it unconditionally. Others made a distinction between the leadership of JP's movement, which they saw as reactionary and pro-American in the main, and the masses who joined it as an outlet for their growing discontent and frustration with the hollow populism of the Congress government.

Indeed it was this growing discontent, which had its roots in the profound economic crisis in the country, that was a much more real threat in the long run to the established order than JP's movement which, after all, was never concerned with the basic issues facing the people—bread and land.

The economic crisis, arising basically out of an outmoded agrarian structure leading to stagnation in both industry and agriculture, and to acute inflation and unemployment as a result, forced a political crisis too, with increasingly authoritarian and repressive measures against the people, 68% of whom were living below the breadline in 1975. This single fact speaks volumes about the socialism vaunted by Indira Gandhi. Indeed, since independence, the numbers driven below the poverty live have increased steadily and relentlessly.

The socialist measures announced by Mrs Gandhi after the Congress Party split in 1969, stood revealed for what they were long before the emergency.

Bank nationalisation in 1969 was the first of these, albeit of Indian banks only. Foreign banks which have been ploughing back millions to their home countries, were untouched. But bank nationalisation effectively favoured big industry and rich farmers above all, being able to channelize credit in a far more concentrated and organised way than before. The "small man" for whom this measure was ostensibly intended, lost out heavily on all sides for the most part. Banking mentality in the State banks continued to be conservative and profit oriented, making it impossible for anyone without sufficient guarantee of repayment to benefit from the new set up. Those from the "weaker sections" (for whom bank nationalisation was proclaimed,) who did manage to scrape up a respectable guarantee in the form of movable or immovable property, were then landed with the problem of paying back the loan compulsorily, on the due date of return or suffering attachment of their property—or jail if they failed. These sections, traditionally dependant on the much more exploitative but lax money lenders, were ruined by their inability to pay back at the appointed hour, especially as many of them had been forced to spend the money to meet expenses quite other than what the loan was intended for.

The complaint for government officials and bankers was that this "non-productive" expenditure was on items like marriages, festivals and deaths. However, as was revealed to us in the villages of Mehrauli (a microcosm), was that a loan of Rs 2000 to a landless Harijan for the purchase of a buffalo, or to build a house with, dwindled to less than Rs 500 in hand by the time he had paid off the various official intermediaries from government to bloc to *panchayat*, each of whom had to have his cut before he would move the papers on to the next stage for realisation of the loan. Faced by his creditors a year later, he was compelled to run to the very money lender from whose clutches the nationalised banks were to have saved him.

When the feudal princes had their privy purses cancelled in 1971, the compensation to them, paid out of the public exchequer, was on a scale to make a nonsense of the cancellation. So too with the nationalisation of coal in 1973. The coal industry had hitherto been mainly in the hands of indigenous, small and middle industrialists. The price of coal was relatively cheap and available at a uniform price to all. When the government stepped in and nationalised coal, the price increased by three to four times for the ordinary consumer, but was heavily subsidised for big industry.

All these measures and many more, especially for example, the intensification of the drive for export oriented industry, for which again heavy subsidies in the form of cheap rates, tax concessions and low-interest credit etc. were generous, led to an increasing deficit on the one hand, and an increasing rate of indirect taxation of the people on the other. 75% of the budget came from indirect taxes by 1975. That is on the price of goods and services essential for the common man.

With 88% of the national work force being in the unorganised sector, both in industry and in agriculture, and thus unprotected and precariously insecure, it is clear which sections of society suffered most from Mrs Gandhi's socialism—the unemployed, the under-employed and the unorganised, in a word, those very 'weaker sections' so cherished by her.

It should be equally clear which sections benefited. And between the oppressors and the oppressed stood the hard pressed and frustrated middle classes, striving to maintain a status quo which was being undermined at its very root by the self-same economic crisis faced by the masses of the people, but unable to see that its salvation lay in joining hands with these masses in a common struggle for a better existence. Hence too, the failure of JP's movement.

The discontent, anger and resistance of the people was as inevitable as the authoritarian measures unleashed against them by the government. An example was the ruthless terror employed against the striking railwaymen and their families in the railway strike of 1974, and also in the determination to stamp out and crush every sign and form of resistance or protest in the downtrodden masses. The political crisis manifested itself in the ruling party itself, with rival factions becoming increasingly vocal, various lobbies pulling in different directions, and the Centre finding it hard to hold together and cope with the general chaos.

When the Allahabad High Court judgement was made against Mrs Gandhi, and the charges of electoral malpractices brought against her by her rival Raj Narain of the BLD, were upheld by Mr Justice Sinha, disqualifying her from office for six years, it was imperative that she make a quick and drastic decision either to step down or to clamp down. She decided on the latter and declared the state of emergency on 26 June.

In an obviously pre-planned and well prepared move, almost the entire opposition consisting of all the parliamentary and non-parliamentary parties and groups who opposed Mrs Gandhi, various social workers, journalists and others critical of her were rounded up in a pre-dawn swoop by the police all over the country that day, and in the daily arrests that followed. Thousands of people were held incommunicado under the MISA and the Defence of India Rules (DIR) preventive detention laws. A number of political organisations said to be 'extremist', such as the RSS, the Anand Marg (a religious sect), the Muslim Majlis and Jamaat-e-Islami and all the Maoist groups were banned. Press censorship was ordered and the right of appeal in the courts was suspended. All dissent was crushed.

The newspapers and radio gave daily reports of the situation as the government saw it. Mrs Gandhi compared herself to Salvador Allende and insisted that "dark forces of reaction" were out to destroy her too. She announced a 20-Point Programme to lead the country back from economic chaos. Denying that she was bent only on preserving her own 'chair' or power, and stifling all opposition, she repeatedly said that only a handful of the people arrested were political, the vast majority being smugglers, black-marketeers, and 'anti-social' elements.

The 20-Point Programme announced on 1 July 1975 became the key *mantra* or slogan for the Congress government. This along with clarion calls for 'discipline', soon revealed the contradictions in a dictatorship which cloaks itself in populism.

The 20-Point Programme included such radical slogans as the liquidation of rural debt, the elimination of bonded labour, the revision and enhancement of minimum wages for agricultural labour and the speedy distribution of surplus land to the landless under the land ceiling act. If implemented, these slogans

would have gone a long way in removing the basic constraints on
the economy which were holding us back. But these slogans have
been part of every Congress programme since 1934, and every
five-year plan since independence. However, except for 'refinements' which have in fact watered down the essentials over the
years, they have remained paper slogans throughout, and to date
even the minimum requirements for their fulfilment, in the form
of proper records of land ownership and tenancy, have not been
completed.

Other points in the Programme included the waiving of
income tax for annual incomes of up to Rs 8,000, aimed as relief
to the hard-pressed middle classes, a new scheme for the "more
effective participation of workers in industries", and liberalisation
of investment procedures and import licensing.

On paper, the 20-Point Programme was as radical and
comprehensive as one could expect. But, reading the rare newspapers and weeklies (like the *Indian Express* and the *Economic
and Political Weekly*) which maintained their independence and
integrity despite enormous pressure and harrassment from the
government, it soon became clear which aspects of it were meant
as window-dressing and which were meant in earnest. The first
moves were to make the scheme for "more effective participation
of workers in industries" a success. This was accomplished by
suspending all basic trade union rights and activity. The trade
union leaders not affiliated to either the Congress-led Indian
National Trade Union Congress (INTUC) or the CPI-led All
India Trade Union Congress (AITUC) were either arrested or
hounded into submission. Having curbed the workers, the
government moved on to give effect to its liberalisation policy
towards industry—both Indian and foreign. It announced a
series of incentives in the form of relaxed taxation and import
duties, dilution of equity holdings for foreign capital, especially
in export-oriented industries, and removal of the "inhibiting"
curbs on licenses and monopolies.

Big industry recorded its pleasure by approving the state of
emergency in the annual meeting of the Federation of Indian
Chambers of Commerce and Industry (FICCI), and delegations
of foreign businessmen from Britain, West Germany, the USA
and other countries poured into India and also expressed their
satisfaction at the direction the government's economic policies

were taking. The final blessing was of course given later. After
the launching of the forced sterilisation campaign by the government, Robert McNamara of the World Bank pronounced that
India had indeed earned the right to more foreign aid. So much
for Mrs Gandhi's 'socialism', a pretence given some credence by
the backing of the Soviet Union and the CPI. One wonders who
was fooling whom!

"Discipline" was the other *mantra* or slogan. Although it was
proclaimed as an offensive against corruption, sloth and ineffi-
ciency, it soon became clear what the real content of this
"discipline" was. When the landless peasants demanded the
distribution of surplus land according to the 20-Point Programme and had their huts burned down by angry landlords, the
police fired on the peasants to "keep order". When agricultural
labourers demanded the newly-announced minimum wages,
they were *lathi-charged* and taken to prison. When workers
demanded the restoration of their wages frozen under the crip-
pling Compulsory Deposit Scheme which was to have come to
an end in 1975, they were ruthlessly suppressed. All in the name
of "discipline".

So too was it a case of "discipline" when some conscientious
district commissioner naively tried to implement the measures
under the 20-Point Programme in his district. He merely
antagonised the local vested interests who, being either Congressmen themselves or relatives of Congressmen, soon had him
transferred out of the district to some remote corner of the
country for his pains. In fact it was business as usual with an
added punch.

As this "discipline" got under way, the naked face of fascism
became exposed. Under the slogan "Clean Up the Cities",
whole slums were bulldozed overnight, wrecking the homesteads
and even the pitiful savings of the inhabitants while they themselves were sterilized and summarily shipped off to new settle-
ments miles outside the city and away from their places of
work. Not only were they cut off from all source of livelihood,
but the much-vaunted resettlement colonies lacked all the basic
facilities of water, drains, electricity, schools, and transport.
Moreover, most of the buildings these people were herded
into were incomplete and did not even have roofs. Such were
the resettlement schemes lauded in the media as a "new deal".

for slum-dwellers. One or two of these were indeed completed
and put on show for foreign visitors like Margaret Thatcher
and Jennie Lee who were duly impressed.

When the slum-dwellers, made desperate by the prospect of
being removed so far out of the way from their places of work
and with no means of getting to them either, refused to move,
they were bulldozed too. The most notorious case was in Delhi
itself, at Turkman Gate, and even the gagged press could not
suppress the news.

The beggars of Bombay were similarly swept out and herded
into camps well out of the way of visiting foreigners. But beggars are a wily lot. Most of them escaped and found their
way back to their old haunts and the keenest of Mrs Gandhi's
officials did not have the energy to track them down again.

Whole buildings worth millions were torn down to clear up
the crowded bazaars of the cities, ruining the small shopkeepers
and traders who had put their life's savings into these homes
and shops they had built for themselves. These were termed
"illegal structures", as indeed they probably were in the municipal blueprints, just as the slums too were illegal. But apart
from the fact that all these illegal squatters had been legalised
by this very government by virtue of their registration on voters
lists and provision by the municipalities of water, electricity
and transport, not to speak of promises of more facilities by
politicians out for their votes, the whole problem of urban over-
population and all its attendant sores in the cities of India
is surely not a legal one at all. It is endemic in a system which
drives the impoverished and landless rural millions into the
cities for employment, forcing them to live and die like pariahs
in the streets. Tucking them away into resettlement colonies
without giving them productive employment is no answer.

The sterilisation campaign was perhaps resorted to as the last
step before the "final solution". Here again the indignity and
brutality inflicted on the people compelled them to resist in
many parts of the country. In Muzzafarnagar in the state of
Uttar Pradesh, hundreds of unarmed men and women were shot
down by the police when they demonstrated against the forced
sterilisations. This time even the rubber-stamp parliament was
forced to ask a few questions and Mrs Gandhi reluctantly

admitted that "only" forty four people had been killed in the police shooting.

All this in the name of "discipline". And much more, much worse. Personal vindictiveness, political revenge, blatant malice, corruption, lies and the lust for power had free reign under this discipline. And it was wielded not only by the forces of law and order, but by every Congress hack and lackey who held the people in terror by virtue of his unrestricted power under the emergency.

It must be said after all this that in the first few months of the emergency there was indeed an improvement on some fronts. The fall in prices of essential goods was the chief of these, and the most needed, but there was also an increase in punctuality and efficiency in some government departments and in transport and other public services. "Trains are running on time," was a frequent and appreciative comment. But all the basic problems remained, and these superficial improvements brought about by threat and under fear, soon failed to halt the slide back into the old state of affairs.

In the last analysis I think it would be correct to say that the emergency was a measure forced upon a government which had nothing else to give its people. Mrs Gandhi however was not peculiar or unique in her despotism. Listening to the BBC on my transistor in jail was salutary. There were similar 'emergencies' concurrently in Sri Lanka, Bangladesh, Burma, Pakistan, Indonesia, Malaysia and the Philippines, to look no further. If it wasn't one party rule under an emergency it was martial law. You could take your pick.

2

"Why is it that so many workers live in unspeakable misery? With their hands they have built great cities, and they cannot be sure of a roof over their heads. With their hands they have opened mines and dragged forth with the strength of their bodies the buried sunshine of the forests, and they are cold. They have gone down into the bowels of the earth for diamonds and gold, and they haggle for a loaf of bread. With their hands they erect temple and palace, and their habitation is a crowded room. . . . They plow and sow and fill our hands with flowers . . . . Their own hands are full of husks."

Helen Keller, quoted in a letter from a friend.

I WOULD LIKE TO DESCRIBE IN SOME DETAIL THE NATURE of our life and work in Mehrauli, in the southern out-skirts of the city of Delhi. It was here that, in a struggle for the legal rights of various sections of rural workers, particularly farm workers, we had organised the Dehat Mazdoor Union (Rural Workers Union). This was a struggle which culminated in the arrest and detention of Srilata and myself under MISA, and of twelve other members of our Executive Committee, all workers, under the Defence of India rules, from which they were released on bail after three months.

Our experience was not peculiar or unique, and comprised but a small part of the experience of the dispossessed all over India. But it did expose the reality behind the facade of the radical slogans which had filled the air ever since Mrs Gandhi assumed power in 1966. Indeed, it was partly under the influence of her famous *"Garibi Hatao"* (Remove Poverty) programme of 1971, that our work began. Experience taught us however, that all these radical slogans and even the legislation that was passed in the interests of the "weaker sections" of the people, remained merely promises on paper. Anyone who had the temerity to try and implement any such legislation soon found that out. And the antagonism aroused, the repression brought down on the weakest of these "weaker sections", the hitherto unorganised and scattered rural poor, was an object lesson in the politics of populism.

The propaganda of the 20-Point Programme let loose on the

country after the declaration of the emergency was therefore
especially ironic for those of us who had been struggling for the
very same things in practice, and had found overselves in prison
as a result.

We came to Delhi from Bombay in the winter of 1971.
Charles, who works for a publishing firm, was going to set
up the head office in Delhi. With us were Karoki and Rita,
a young girl from Mangalore who had worked for us in Bombay
and decided to come to Delhi with us as well. The year in
Bombay had opened my eyes to life in the slums of the city.
When we moved to Delhi we wanted to live simply, more
in tune with the reality of the country and away, if possible, from
the pretentious residential "colonies" of Delhi's upper class elite.

Some friends who had a farm beyond the Qutab Minar in the
Mehrauli *tehsil* or district of south Delhi, wanted to rent out
their farmhouse and we were glad to take up their offer. It was
a delightful place, built on traditional village lines and surrounded by four acres of orchards and fields. The little village school
across the field in front of our house seemed an ideal place
for Karoki to begin his Indianisation, and we settled in happily.

Our neighbours were a mixed lot. The village closest to us was
called Gadaipur. It was dominated (economically) by a few
Sindhi families, refugees from Pakistan in 1947. The rest of the
population was composed of extremely poor Muslims and
harijans in the main. Neighbouring villages like Sultanpur,
Jaunapur, and Mandi near the Haryana border were dominated
by the tough Jat and Gujar castes. The former were traditionally
peasants but they had now taken to contracting and other business
in the area; the latter were originally bandits who had settled over
the years into herding cattle and running dairy farms, and were
now also into the contracting business in the stone and sand
quarries and brickworks dotted all over that area. The rest of
the population in these villages consisted mainly of harijans
'untouchables' with a sprinkling of Brahmins, Muslims and
other castes.

The villagers had sold most of their land very cheaply some
fifteen or twenty years before to the Delhi Development Authority (DDA). The DDA had then auctioned it off at prices
ranging between Rs 4,000 to Rs 6,000 an acre to members of
the urban gentry. We were dismayed to find that our search for

simplicity had landed us among the cream of the country's elite. The landowners here included five-star generals, top industrialists like Tata, Birla, Dalmia, Charat Ram and Bharat Ram, several rajas and maharajas, and a number of politicians, including the Prime Minister Mrs Gandhi, the Minister for Petroleum and Fuels, Mr K.D. Malaviya, and the Minister for Agriculture, Mr Jagjivan Ram. Apart from these there were also senior officials like Mr B. K. Nehru, then Indian High Commissioner in London, and scores of other important bureaucrats and businessmen.

The land, which had been largely unproductive in the past for lack of sufficient irrigation and transport facilities, was now developed quickly. Roads were built, electricity was laid down and tubewells were sunk to reach the abundant subsoil water hitherto untapped by the villagers for lack of resources. The real boom, however, was not so much in agriculture, an activity in which the sophisticated urban elite was not overly interested, but in real estate speculation and the opportunity which tax-free agriculture offered to turn black money into white. Land values soared and at the time when we arrived there the price of an acre of developed land was above Rs 40,000.

Most of the owners were absentee landlords living in distant places like Bombay and Calcutta, London, Paris, Tokyo and New York. As a result of this a number of the farms lay fallow. In addition many of the large mansions that had been built as country retreats or pleasure spots remained empty. But other farms thrived with the production of fruits such as grapes, peaches, oranges, grapefruits and melons, garden vegetables. and crops such as wheat, rice, maize and barley. Some of the farmers had actually moved into the countryside and had taken to farming seriously. Most of these also ran dairies, poultry farms and allied industries. The production of high quality roses was another flourishing business, the blooms being exported to Europe by air.

The local villagers, especially the peasants who had sold their land so cheaply, were, as we soon learned, bitter about the boom they had witnessed here. They felt cheated and said that if they had been given the facilities of irrigation and transport etc., which had been made available to the gentlemen farmers so quickly, they would never have parted with their land.

Mehrauli was a VIP area, but the improvements which had been effected for the VIP's had left the villages surrounding their farms almost untouched. Conditions here were as backward and 'simple' as in the remotest parts of the country. But of that, later.

The workers on the farms, the *malis* (gardeners) as they were called, were all immigrants from eastern Uttar Pradesh known as *purabias* (Easterners). The farm owners, being absentee landlords, could not trust the local villagers to work on and guard their farms. The risk of constant pilferage was one consideration, but more serious by far was the danger that these dispossessed villagers might make a claim to the land that had once been theirs under the new tenancy laws, especially as most of them wanted to work as share croppers rather than as wage workers. The *purabias*, however, were no threat at all. Driven by hunger and debt from their villages, they had flocked to the city and were grateful for any crumbs that came their way. A more malnourished, tattered, wretched looking lot would have been hard to find.

Our farm was called *Bagh Dil-Bagh*, meaning something like "garden of the heart". It was not really 'our' farm, as we had only rented the farmhouse, but it soon came to feel like ours. Working on the farm were two full-time resident *malis* employed by the owners. One was called Nandkoo, a tall gentle faced young man. With him were his beautiful wife Ram Pyari and their little daughter, a wild, black imp of a girl whose name was Ramlalli but whom we all called Munni. She was just about Karoki's age and friendship between them was immediate. The other *mali* was Parlad, single (his family had been left behind in the village), stocky, rather fey and very easygoing. There was a share cropper on this farm as well. His name was Bacchan Lal and he insisted that he was a "Bahmin" or brahmin, although everyone seemed sceptical about this claim. His wife, whom we called *Mataji* or mother, and their two children, Shyamlal, a boy of about twelve and a girl of eight, also called Munni, soon became part of the family and appropriated Karoki as well.

Karoki and Nandkoo's little daughter soon began going off to school together, their *takhtis*, or wooden writing boards, clutched under their arms. The teachers were intrigued but took the new infants in their stride. Karoki may have learned little academically beyond some excellent *dehati* or village Hindi and a string of scorching swear words, but he had a wonderful year at school. The house was soon flooded with his friends—village children, curious and shy at first, then rowdy and hard to restrain. After a while Karoki spent as much time in their homes as they did in his. But Munni, Nandkoo's Munni was his favourite. They slept, ate, and played together, stole sweets and told lies together, went exploring and got stuck in thorn bushes and snake holes together. And when, some six months after our arrival, Nandkoo had to take his wife and daughter home as he could not afford to keep them with him any longer, Karoki was heartbroken, as indeed we all were. Shining, wicked, wilful little Munni. What a woman she could have grown to be, but what chance did she have? What chance was there for her in life?

We had a sprinkling of the farm-owning gentry around us, but we tried to steer clear of them. We had not come so far out of the way to fall into the old life style again. On our immediate left was an eight-acre farm owned by Air Marshal Arjan Singh, ex-chief of the Air Staff, and at the time, Indian Ambassador in France. Beyond his farm were the opulent double-storeyed mansions of the Kapoor brothers, big businessmen who lived out here and were expanding both in industry and in agriculture in this area. Strictly speaking this was part of the green belt of the city of Delhi, and no factories nor anything above single-storeyed buildings could be erected in the entire area, but who could deny anything to the VIP's? Round the corner from the Kapoor brothers were the farms of Generals Rawley and Bhatia, and opposite them the huge estate of the *Rajmata* of Jodhpur. Then there was the flourishing ashram of a strapping Sikh *maharaj* or guru who held court every day to streams of devotees, mostly women, and several rich ones who kept him supplied with air-conditioners, refrigerators, automobiles and whatever else His Holiness fancied.

With Charles miles away in office all day, I had plenty of time to get to know our neighbours, and so, shrinking from the Kapoor's and their like, I began to exploit to the full this chance to get to know, to experience, and to understand something of village India.

My first friends were the Nandkoo's and Parlad. I used to watch them in the fields, tending the fruit trees, chopping the *chara* or fodder for the cow, milking it and cleaning up its dung which they made into cakes and dried in the sun for fuel. They had one tiny room each, by the side of the cow, and I used to sit with them while they cooked their food on their little *angithis* or braziers, using sticks and leaves and straw for fuel when they ran out of dung. They were paid approximately eighty rupees each a month without food or any other benefits. Their working hours began before sunrise and ended well after sunset each day. Nandkoo was a serious and very hardworking man, but Parlad was always ready for a bit of gossip. His kohl-darkened, wicked little eyes would light up at the chance to squat back on his haunches, put down his *khurpi* (a digging tool) light up a *bidi*, roll a weed of *bhang* or marijuana and tell his tales of woe and joy for hours on end.

With winter colder by several degrees out here in the country than in the city, I found they had nothing warm to wear. Munni of course came in for Karoki's clothes and her mother did quite well out of me, but the men had nothing. They came to me one evening and said they were ashamed even to ask, but could I loan them twenty rupees each to buy something to keep out the cold. I gave them the money, sure that it would never be returned. They each bought themselves a stout pair of trousers from the pavement bazaar which was held every Sunday at the foot of Jama Masjid in the old city of Delhi. I went there myself one Sunday morning soon after and bought them two thick woollen Swedish air force jackets for a song. Nandkoo and Parlad looked like something out of a magazine in their new clothes and were quite overwhelmed that I, who did not even employ them, should have been "so generous" when their own *sahib* could not have cared less about them. I tried to explain that this, and indeed much more than this, was their rightful due and that it was no favour that they should have it, but they could only fold their hands in gratitude and say that I was a *mahatma*, or great soul indeed! At the start of the next month when they received their pay, Nandkoo and Parlad came to me with the money they had borrowed. I was surprised and moved. It was a quarter of their monthly income and yet they had not hesitated or 'forgotten' to return it, as I had expected. I told them to keep it, and wondered how I could express some of the thoughts that arose in my mind. Thoughts about the contradictions in life where those who work like dogs from morning to night have to beg for the clothes on their back, but whose natural pride and self-respect has still not died within them.

I began to realise how expendable, how cheap, how worthless, human labour was. They simply did not count, these sweating, toiling, ragged *purabias*. There were hundreds, thousands, millions like them. Squeeze one dry and cast him out, then suck another and another—there were no shortages here at any rate.

Nandkoo and Parlad never heard a word of appreciation for work done well. Only the harsh, shrill voice of suspicion and abuse whenever their *malik* or employer descended on them from time to time to see how things were going. We began to find the warmth and courtesy of their employers towards us intolerable when we saw how they treated our friends who worked like serfs for them. They would rather see vegetables and fruit on their farm rot and fall to the ground for worms and sparrows to eat than allow one of their *maliks* to take a handful, even for his child.

And then one day, the mistress of the farm came on a visit. Irritated with something Parlad had said or done she caught hold of him by the ear, marched him to his hut, bade him gather up his belongings and cursing him roundly, threw him out of the farm. Although he had worked for her for two years, there was no settlement of dues, no notice, no warning. We were all shaken, and Nandkoo was bitter. He told us that this job on the farm, ill-paid as it was, was still a relatively comfortable and secure one for the *purabia*. The alternative was to become a *deharidar* or daily-wage labourer, earning three or four rupees a day if lucky, for a gruelling day's work, uncertain of the next day's meal, knocked about without shelter, livelihood, and living from hand to mouth. This was Parlad's fate—a fate shared by thousands of his fellow *purabias* here, and millionᵉ everywhere else in India.

Till now I had only second-hand knowledge (gained through
books and newspapers, and a little through the work I had done
in the slums of Bombay), of these things—poverty, hunger,
unemployment—but here, living among the very victims themselves, I came to see, to feel, and to realise concretely what it
meant. I never saw Parlad again.

Through Nandkoo and Parlad I had come to know their
friends, our other neighbours. On our right was Ram Pher. He
lived with his wife and two small sons on a bare uncultivated
patch of land that belonged to an absentee farmer. Ram Pher
was paid a monthly salary of a hundred rupees. But he was not
paid every month; his *malik* came to Delhi once every four or
five months on business, and Ram Pher was paid his dues then.
In the meanwhile he had to fend for himself, borrowing money
from money lenders to keep himself and his family alive. The
interest? That was his affairs; the *malik* was not concerned. But
he was forbidden to grow any vegetables for his own use on the
land. I met the *malik* once, and asked him why Ram Pher
couldn't be allowed to grow just a few things with which to feed
himself and his family.

"No fear!" said the *malik*. "You will give these people ideas
with talk like that! If you give them an inch they'll take over
your whole farm under these stupid tenancy laws."

The new tenancy laws proclaimed that a tiller of the soil
could lay claim to any land which he had tilled for three con-
secutive years. Most of the *purabias* were ignorant of this law
and none of them had the courage anyway to make such a
claim. The farm owners, most of whom had not bothered even
to register their farms and certainly not to register their
employees as wage workers, were taking no risks.

Ram Pher was a highly intelligent man, totally unread (here
in these areas illiteracy stood at 99%), extremely sensitive and
quick to grasp new ideas. But he was also a timid man who lived
in constant dread of all those who were mighty and could crush
him without any effort, if he as much as dared to raise his head
too high. First, his *malik*—Ram Pher could not, he *would* not
dare even to suggest that he be paid his wages every month so
that he could avoid falling into debt. The Gujar and Jat upper
castes were next in his daily round of fear. Living, as he said
time and again, just on the edge of the main road to the villages

of Jaunapur and Mandi, both of which were notorious for brigands and other lawless elements especially among the Jats and Gujars, he was exposed and defenceless against any attack they might choose to make on his wife's honour or her life's savings in silver bangles, his master's tubewell engine, or on them all, simply for the sport of terrorising 'untouchables'. For all the *purabias* were in this category—harijans, to use Gandhi's term for them. Other fears which Ram Pher harboured were for the safety of his two small sons, the eldest barely two years old. The well in front of his hut was a constant danger, its walls being just low enough for both the little toddlers to scramble over. There was no light either, as his master refused to provide him with a bulb and he could ill afford one himself. So he lived in the dark, in mortal fear of the well and the villagers, and of the snakes which posed yet another threat—this patient, frightened man who was so full of humour and intelligence in spite of everything.

The Air Marshal's farm, and the one just opposite it which belonged to a Mr Malhotra, were looked after by the brothers Rameshwar and Ramnath respectively. A long-standing feud between their wives back at home was a constant source of tension between them and of hilarity for all their friends. Rameshwar was slow-moving and big, an easygoing *bhang* addict. Ramnath was quick, sharp, a superb gardener, and he had a nice little savings account in the bank which was not only the envy of his brother but of all the *purabias* in the area. Ramnath was such a good worker that his *malik* looked after him relatively well, and being thrifty Ramnath had managed to save a little money every month with which he later opened a small tea shop. With this he was well on the way to independence. Mr Malhotra was a rare employer, and even though Ramnath became one of the most active workers in the Union we eventually organised, he was never harassed or intimidated by his employer as a result.

But Ramnath and Rameshwar were at daggers drawn, and many were the informal *panchayats* or meetings that were held to restore peace between them. This was something I noticed among the *purabias*—their readiness to fly at each other's throat at the least hint of an insult or abuse. The strife and quarrelling over little things, the fierce protection of their *izzat* or honour, were especially striking when I saw how they submitted so abjectly to the insults, brutality and callousness of their *maliks* and all the petty officials they came in contact with. This latter they accepted as their 'fate', but let one *purabia* insult another and blood could flow.

The harm they did themselves, blind as they were to the real cause of their festering resentments and humiliation, came home to me concretely as I began to take part in their lives.

Time and again I noticed this confusion in the *purabia's* mind. Constant humiliation at the hands of his 'superiors' made him extra sensitive to the least suggestion of insult from his equals. He reacted to the latter violently and blindly, injuring himself twice over as a result. The case of Sriram will suffice as an example.

Sriram, a big, broad, shy young fellow, worked as a *mali* and *chowkidar* on a farm not far from where we lived, and was one of the first friends we made. He was involved in an expensive court case which was a drain on his meagre earnings of a hundred rupees a month. It all began with a quarrel over a *dholak* for a *kirtan*, the one social event in the immigrant *purabia's* life. It seems that Sriram, who was invited to the *kirtan* had refused to lend his *dholak* for the occasion. The irate party who had come to borrow it was so incensed that he bribed the local police to register a case against Sriram for allegedly brewing illicit liquor on his farm. Two empty bottles of spirit were "recovered" from behind some bushes and the case was established. Sriram did not even drink, but that was irrelevant. When I came on the scene the case was three years old and as yet the police had not even brought forward their evidence. But Sriram was forced to appear in court once every three weeks all these years. Each appearance meant a long bus ride into town, the criminal courts in Parliament Street being about 12 miles away, a day's wages lost, either no food or added expense incurred for any refreshments, and a long, weary wait. Perhaps his name would not be called until late afternoon although he was required to arrive punctually at 10 a.m. each time, and all he got on being summoned into the presence of the magistrate was another date for the hearing three weeks later. It was impossible to get home after this by bus once the evening office rush had started, the buses were all full, so often he had to walk the long distance back, and then cook himself a meal at the end of it before he could go to sleep.

Sriram's lawyer, a shark like most of the lawyers in the criminal courts, took money off him every month although this was against the original arrangement by which he had been paid a lump sum for the whole case, money which Sriram had had to borrow in the first place. The lawyer was in no hurry to finish the case. As long as it continued he was assured of a regular income. He had innumerable clients like Sriram. When I went with him to the courts, my first ever visit there, I found the lawyer's room crowded with folk like Sriram, illiterate, impoverished and at the mercy of the lawyer's demands. They had to beg, borrow and even steal in order to pay him because he would lose interest in fighting their cases if they did not keep him happy.

Outraged, I went to see the Sub-divisional Magistrate (SDM) for Mehrauli. A petite young woman sitting behind the huge desk on the magistrate's dais looked up and smiled. She asked me to wait in her office, she would be with me in a moment. When she came she said, "You don't recognise me—I was your student at Indraprastha College. Aruna Roy—English Honours."

"Good Lord," I said, "Of course!"

I told her what the problem was and she shook her head.

"These lawyers are all crooks," she said, "and the judges in these lower courts are not much better! But go and see Mr Jain." She gave me a note for him, "He is a good lawyer, and clean, and I don't think he will charge you too much."

Sriram and I found Mr Jain from among the lawyers' bazaar which sprawls around the courts, and he agreed to take on the case for forty rupees. He nodded his head sympathetically when we told him of our experiences at the hands of his colleague, and said it was sad that his brethren were so exploitative of the ignorant and the poor. Within a month the case was over, dismissed, and Sriram was aquitted. All it needed was for two witnesses to say that they had seen the "other party" putting the bottles of spirit behind the bushes on Sriram's farm.

That was my first encounter with the law. I had tried to give

the new lawyer details of the case, to tell him the truth of what
had happened. He laughed at me and said, "Mrs Lewis, the
law isn't concerned with the truth, it is only concerned with
evidence."

The truth of his words was to be proved again and again, but
at the time I could only wonder.

There was so much talk about legal aid for the poor. Commission after commission of judges, lawyers, and civil servants
had produced their reports stressing the absolute necessity for
this. The Congress government lost no chance of promising free
legal aid to the poor, but these promises were never fulfilled.
Later under the emergency, slogans about legal aid for the poor
were shouted louder than ever; it was admitted (as before) that
justice could only be bought in our country and that it was
beyond the means of 80% of our people, but this like other
slogans was meant to remain on paper, or in the air. Even now,
at the lime of writing, no steps have been taken to effect this and
the people continue to be oppressed by a system of justice in
which all the dice are loaded against them if they are poor.

But in 1972, as I began to discover, it was not only the
system of justice that was loaded against the poor. Everything,
every institution, even the institutions which had been built
ostensibly for the poor on public funds, such as government
hospitals, clinics, postal services all worked against them.

Take the case of Hiralal. He was an elderly man with a
worn-looking wife and two beautiful children. He had worked
on a farm for twenty years and was paid just over a hundred
rupees a month. Hiralal had scraped and saved over the years
and had recently bought a cow and a calf. These were his sole
possessions and he loved them as his own children. One day his
daughter took the calf out and got into a fight with "that
Musalman from Gadaipur" (we never knew which one). The
Muslim apparently hit the calf across the back with his *lathi.*
The blow seemed to have broken its spine and it was seriously
ill when Hiralal came to me.

"*Behnji*, please come with me to the animal hospital. If my
calf dies I will be ruined and no one there will listen to me if
you don't come with me," he said.

I went with him to Mehrauli. The government veterinary clinic
was just opposite the Block Development Office (BDO). It was

after 11 a.m. We entered a large courtyard in the middle of a sprawling old building on one side of which was the hospital, the other side being the doctor's quarters. In a stall by the side of the doctor's residence were five or six sleek and well-kept buffaloes. They belonged to the "doctor sahib," we were told.

"Where is the doctor sahib?" I asked a sleepy looking, shifty-eyed clerk who turned out to be the vet's assistant as well.

"He's not come yet," he said.

"Well this man's calf is desperately ill and needs immediate attention."

I told him what had happened. He shrugged, "It's only because you have come with this fellow that I haven't thrown him out of this place—we have no time for the likes of him."

"But why? Isn't this a public hospital?" I asked.

"Yes, yes," he answered tiredly, "of course it is. But who is the public? Do you think it is people like this? We get calls from generals and ministers here. They pay us ten rupees a visit and send their cars for us. How can we attend to people like this? They have no money, no transport, no nothing."

"But for goodness' sake, it's your duty. You are supposed to dispense free medical aid here and this hospital is specially meant for those who can't afford to pay private fees. You are supposed to provide free medicines as well."

He winked at me. "Come, I'll show you what we are *supposed* to do!" I followed him inside. On the wall in the office was a large map of the Mehrauli *tehsil*.

"This is our area," he pointed to it. "The doctor is supposed to patrol this entire area himself. The World Health Organisation has even given us a jeep for the purpose. . . ."

"Then why?"

He winked again, "Come and look." He took me outside and pointed to a land rover, dented, broken down, with no wheels, lying in a heap in the sun in a corner of the compound. That is our transport!"

"An accident?" I queried.

"Forget it. Sheer disuse. It came new and got like that standing there in the sun and rain. Who bothers? *Sarkar ka mal hai*." He was quite candid, he didn't even try to cover up. Medicines? The government sent supplies now and again but they usually ran out before the next lot came.

"And anyway," he said. "You see those buffaloes? Healthy aren't they! And then we have so *many* obligations—the sahibs on the farms must get the best. For these poor fellows—well, it's safer to buy what they need in the market."

By the time the vet arrived I was angry and showed it.

"There, there madam, I'm here to help you," he tried to be soothing. "It is our duty to help people like you."

"People like me can bloody well go to private vets," I told him. "It's people like *him* you're here to help."

He wanted to know the details, which Hiralal told him, standing with hands folded, begging him to save his calf. When the vet hemmed and hawed I told him he had better send a man to see to the calf at once or I would report him to the BDO next door.

The vet's assistant came for five days running to give the calf injections which we had had to buy from the chemist after all, having been warned by the vet that it was the only way we could be sure of getting unadulterated vaccine. But the calf died anyway, and with it dead the cow was useless for milk and Hiralal had to get rid of it.

As I became acquainted with the villagers and other folk and they found me sympathetic, they began to approach me with some of their problems.

"*Behnji*, we don't want any more children—give us something we can take to stop them coming."

Crowds of village women often surrounded me with this plea.

"But there is a family planning clinic in Mehrauli," I would tell them. "Any public hospital would help you gladly." They would shrink back at that.

"But why?" I asked them, "come on, if you're so frightened I'll take you there myself."

"Not there, *Behnji*, not to the *sarkari ospatal*. We won't come back alive."

Apparently their experience of government hospitals had been bitter, and one bad experience was enough to put off a whole village. Just one messed up case and the whole family planning

effort in a village could be ruined. What kind of things went
wrong? Loops had been fitted without proper explanation or
advice and follow up. When the bleeding and pain started, the
women panicked and rejected the loop. Some of them had had
trouble after getting their tubes tied. The operation was more
serious than they had been led to believe, and of course there was
no aftercare or check-up to see if all was well. The younger
women had another fear. They suspected that if they went to a
government hospital for help they would be secretly sterilised
and they were not ready for this as yet. They said that such cases
were frequent and they were having none of it. So much for
family planning.

But other hospital cases were no different. Time and again I
observed a serious case being rushed to hospital in a taxi. After
a long wait all day the patient would be brought back, again by
taxi, and they would tell me that they had been asked to return
the next day.

It was always the same. No time today, come tomorrow. No
bed today, come tomorrow. No medicines—buy them outside.
But for me? I never had to wait or come back again or be ignored. I was invariably treated courteously, promptly, efficiently. I
always got the medicines prescribed for me. I had always
thought, as I got into my car and drove away, what excellent
public health services we had!

The post office was another public service. Mathura Prasad
had sent his year's savings of ninety rupees to his village by
money order. Some of it was to have gone towards paying his
debt to the moneylender and the rest was for his wife and
children, his old parents and his brothers and sisters in the
village. But the money order never arrived. Mathura went to the
Mehrauli post office with his counterfoil.

"It didn't reach," he told the clerk at the window nervously.

"Oh nonsense. You're telling lies."

"But I never got the acknowledgement."

"Oh go away, get out of here! They're always telling lies,
these people."

A year went by. Mathura tried again and again to track his
money down. Then one day I went with him to the GPO. We
pushed our way into the office of the man in charge of money
orders and made our complaint to him. He promised to check

it up for me. Some two months later the money was delivered to
Mathura's family. The village postman had apparently made off
with the cash and left his job soon after. But villages are small
and it was not difficult to track him down once they got around
to it.

And so on it went. There was no end. I certainly could not
begin to cope with all the problems. Some form of organisation,
cooperative effort and self-help was necessary. This was clear to
all of us. The harijans in the villages were more advanced than
the immigrant workers; most of the men had some education
and held jobs as grade-four government workers in the city.
They had more confidence in themselves and were eager to
improve the deplorable conditions in which they lived. They
suggested we start a self-help programme. We could use their
panchayat ghar or council house. The harijans were not allowed
to use the official *panchayat* house which was the preserve of the
upper castes. They lived apart in their own filthy, swampy
quarter, all the *panchayat* funds and the government aid meant
specially for their welfare going straight into the upper caste
panchayat, for the upkeep of their residential area.

So we began. The Dehat Mazdoor Sudhar Sabha (Rural
Workers Improvement Association) was formed with Sultanpur
village as its headquarters. We would organise night schools, a
rotating fund, a cooperative store, a medical scheme with city
doctors persuaded to give us a few hours of their time once a
week. The harijan youths in the villages were filled with
enthusiasm. Some of them who were college students decided
that they would run the night schools themselves and help to
give the younger children a better education than they could get
in the local primary schools which, they said, discriminated
against harijan children. They were full of zest and spirit.

But the village gentry was hostile. One day the *Pradhan*
observed, "you *chamars* are getting uppity aren't you? So you
have started your own school now; well, we'll see about that.
As for this foolish woman who has filled your heads with all
this nonsense—we'll see about her too!"

The first threats had been made. The harijans were terrified.
Crushed under the weight of casteism, abject 'untouchables'
and outcastes for centuries, they quickly scotched their dreams
for a better life.

"*Behnji*," they said to me, "these people are too powerful. They are dangerous and anything can happen to us if we defy them. We are helpless, no one will listen to us, we dare not go ahead with the plan."

My blood was aroused but I didn't know what to do next. How to make these people move, how to stir, to arouse their crushed humanity? So much was made of the harijans—the scheduled castes and tribes of India—and yet here in the very shadow of the capital city, in the heart of an area framed by the pillars of the state including no less than the Prime Minister herself, was a situation quite medieval in its barbarity. I had thought that such conditions existed only in the remote rural areas of India but the situation of harijans in Delhi was scarcely different.

The upper castes of Sultanpur village deliberately channelled their drain so that it emptied into the compound of the harijan *panchayat*. In the rains a mass of filth spread everywhere; the main road into the harijan section became waist deep in mud and sewage. The children played in the slush. The harijans had tried to block the drain but the upper caste bullies had broken the block and threatened trouble if it was set up again. So the harijans sent petitions to the SDM, the BDO, the District Commissioner (DC) and their local Councillor instead. For seven years their petitions had been doing the rounds but the situation was unchanged.

The harijans of Ghitorni village were accustomed to going for their morning ablutions along a path through the fields of a Jat farmer. The path was marked on the municipal map as a bonafide thoroughfare. But the Jat decided to build a wall along the side of his field and block entry to the path from the village. The harijans now had to walk round by the main road, a distance of some two kilometres, just to relieve themselves. Twelve years of petitioning the authorities had brought plenty of sympathy but no redress. Here too, during the monsoon, the illegally erected wall caused a flood of water to collect in the narrow lane, and this, over the years, had eroded and weakened the foundations of the harijan houses along it and some of them were beginning to crumble.

All the roads and lanes in the harijan quarters of these villages were unpaved, stony dirt tracks. There were no electric posts and the houses too had no electricity. But if you wandered through the residential areas of the upper castes you saw paved, well-lit roads, well-built houses, and the official *panchayat*, a noble building with an immense paved square in front of it. You would find drains dug in every lane here, and if you didn't venture into the harijan section of the village you would go away thinking that great progress had been made.

Among the harijans of Sultanpur and Ghitorni was a small number of fairly well educated men who had managed to acquire a lower middle-class position as primary school teachers, clerks etc., in government departments.

"You should take the lead," I told them. "You can do something to change this situation."

"Hush," I was told. "We dare not. We will never be heard. These people have everything—the *Panchayat Tehsildar*, the Councillors, the police, the District Magistrate. They have the money and the influence, we have nothing."

The leading harijan of Ghitorni village was a gentle, quiet-spoken man whose heart burned with the humiliation of his people, but he was helpless too. His daughter, a minor, had been raped by a Jat landlord who was a relative of the *Pradhan*. He had refused to condone this outrage and gathering every last penny of his savings, begging and borrowing the rest of the money needed, he had taken the Jat to court. Now, he said, he had to remain silent otherwise his case might be affected. The Jat gentry had left no stone unturned in their attempts to trip him up and provoke him into a quarrel or some rash act by which they could prove him to be a trouble maker. They had threatened to burn his house down and drive him out of the village; they had terrorised him and his family at night and threatened further assaults, but he did not dare to raise his voice.

Why? Why? I demanded. Surely this would only strengthen his case?

"You don't understand, *Behnji*," was the patient, gentle answer. "If they can start a quarrel and involve me in a fresh case they can use that as a weapon in the other. They are trying their best to provoke me. They are desperate to mitigate their own crime somehow if they can. Their hands reach very far and they will influence the people who count. It's the only thing," his voice trembled with passion—"it's the only thing I *won't* let happen. I *will* see justice done to my daughter. So I must keep quiet even though they are threatening me and my family all the time—I can't let my children go out after dark or into lonely places for fear of them, but I dare not say anything. The police, you see, are in their pocket."

The tragic thing was that the only form of protest they knew was the ruinous one of going to court. These things which were happening in the capital city itself could surely be brought to public notice? The authorities would surely galvanise themselves into putting a stop to these atrocities? But the problem was to convince these people that *they* must stir themselves and raise their voice against these outrages. I had hoped that the villagers would be less afraid than the immigrants, but I found that when it came to "offending" or falling foul of the old caste hierarchy in the villages these people were just as frightened and timid as the immigrant workers around them.

The migrant labour also came from the scheduled castes and tribes. Their situation, whether on the farms of the urban elite or in the quarries, brickworks, mines and factories nearby owned by lesser gentry from the villages or elsewhere, was the same. Unprotected by any law except that of the jungle, trapped in a thousand ways of indebtedness to their *maliks*, they scratched a bare living from the earth. On as little as two or three rupees a day, they toiled round the clock, injured, blinded, sometimes buried under the falling stones and earth in the mines and quarries. But no voice was ever raised. None of them dared even to notify the police in the event of an accident or death while at work. The *maliks*, wielding life and death powers over them, threatened dire consequences at their least protest. The police and mining inspectors, their palms well greased, turned a blind eye anyway. Who cared for a *"do paise ka purabia?"* He was easily exchanged, expendable.

These immigrants (they described their lives so many times, slowly, painfully, the same story over and over again), had left their villages in the remote areas of Eastern UP, Bihar and Rajasthan, fleeing from landlessness, hunger, debt, unemployment, and flooding the cities in a desperate search for jobs, happy to earn even two rupees a day. This was a fortune compared to the eight and twelve annas they got under total slavery to the *zamindar* or landlord back home. Yet, with this two or

three rupees they had to feed themselves, send some money to
their wives and children in the village and also save enough to
pay back the moneylender from whose clutches they had fled
but who held their families in thrall all the same.

Pardesis or foreigners in this "country", as they called it,
they had no roots here and felt helpless in the face of the hostile
world confronting them. Their jobs, their livelihood, their survival
depended on their absolute submission to their *maliks*. A wrong
step, the slightest mistake made, and they could be thrown
out without a moment's hesitation or notice. Uncertain about
the next day's meal, their life was one of endless subjection,
insecurity and fear.

Outraged by their situation I searched for some way we could
begin to change it. I wanted them to see that it could and must
be changed, but I also realised that with the fear that gripped
them they would need a lot of help and sympathy, not only from
me but from the authorities whom they would doubtless come
in contact with. Surely there were some laws for people like
these? The government made so much noise about harijans,
surely there must be some legal provision for them as well? It
had already become clear to me that our Dehat Mazdoor Sudhar
Sabha, through which we had wanted to start a cooperative and
self-help movement, was not much use to these immigrants
who lived such a precarious existence that their first and desperate need was for some kind of economic security. Finally some
friends suggested that I go to the Ministry of Labour and find
out if there were any laws to protect this section of the people.

I went to the Shram Shakti Bhavan in which the Labour
Ministry was housed, and spoke to the receptionist about the
problem. I told him I wanted specific, concrete answers, not a
lot of hot air. He asked me to wait while he phoned through to
somebody. Then a man came down the stairs and asked me
what I wanted to know. He heard me out, and was plain-
spoken in his reply.

"There are lots of laws," he told me, "that cover such people.
There is the Trade Union Act for a start. . . ."

"Even for agricultural labour?" I asked.

"Yes, it has been extended to them as well. Then there is the
Minimum Wages Act, the Contract Labourers Act, the Factories
Act, the Workman's Compensation Act—but," he looked at me

and shook his head, "none of them is any use at all unless your people are organised. Are they?"

"No."

"Well they won't be heard," he said flatly. "They simply won't be heard. You must organise them. Form a union, fight for their rights. Unless the baby cries how can the mother give it milk?"

I have never forgotten his words.

I went back and gave my friends on the farms the message. Their faces lit up. So we could form a *sarkari* union. We shall register it—have a pad (headed note paper)—an office—a telephone. . . . I cut into their dreams.

"Brothers, let us register what 'union' means amongst ourselves first. The 'pad' and office can come later."

We had to go to the Labour Commissioner's office some twenty miles away in Old Delhi to find out about the rules and regulations for organising a union under the Trade Union Act. The Registrar of Trade Unions was intrigued. This was the first agricultural workers union in Delhi, according to him.

"We've had our eye on your area for some time," he said. "There are thousands of labourers there, but," he spread his hands wide and shrugged, "they are not organised. If you can organise them you will be doing a great work and we will help you in every way we can. But otherwise it is hopeless."

Much encouraged by this support, we called a meeting which was enthusiastically attended, to explain the facts.

Now the apprehensions began. Dreams were all very well, but the reality was that each *purabia mali* (we started with the farm labour as we knew each other best) was terrified. Scattered and spread over a vast area, they were mostly one, seldom more than two or three men, working on a farm. Without the solidarity of a large workforce how would they ever gather the nerve to confront their *maliks* with the announcement, "We have found out about the law. We have certain rights and now we have a union too. We want such and such. . . ." The *malik* would simply kick them out, and who would come to their rescue? *Behnji* couldn't be everywhere at once!

Then began the real slog. The slow, step-by-step struggle

going from farm to farm to make them understand that the Union was not a 'pad' or an office, or *Behnji* waving a magic wand. It was *their* unity, solidarity, organisation, struggle. They alone could win their rights; no *devi* from above (*Behnji*), no official fiat could procure these for them. They would get their rights only through their own collective effort.

But lectures, words, exhortation were all abstractions. These people who had never known, never experienced the rudiments of organisation or collective effort, who had never dreamed of rights, who were completely subjected, would take a long time to learn to stand up.

So we sat together and worked it out, the relatively more enthusiastic among us. We decided to divide up the area into *tolis* or groups of farms neighbouring one another. Each group would meet once a week. In these small group meetings we would explain what 'union' really meant and how we could achieve it. As our message gathered strength we would take up someone's case as a trial, just something small to begin with, to see what happened. The most important thing at this stage was for them to win some confidence in themselves, to begin to perceive their own strength in unity, to solve their own problems together, to resolve their quarrels, differences, animosities collectively and by themselves, instead of running to the police and bringing ruin on all concerned. Through mutual discussion, frankly, freely and openly, we would gradually be able to tackle all our problems, as long as we kept in view the necessity to unite rather than divide, to solve rather than provoke, and to build up trust and friendship amongst ourselves instead of the suspicion, envy, fear and insecurity which now prevailed.

Our Union was not going to be the usual shop-keeping bargain counter that trade unionism had come to mean in our country. It was to be a process of social as well as economic struggle and transformation. We would educate ourselves (literally as well, even learn to read and write) in the fullest sense.

Friends from the city who get to know of what was happening on the farms came to lend a hand. It was a long haul to the Mehrauli *dehat* but some of them, mostly students, were so enthusiastic that they braved the long bus journeys, often staying the night, and helping out in various ways.

We organised a medical scheme, a small group going to the people and others collecting medicines and money from sympathetic friends in the city. A couple of sociology students went from village to village collecting data and finding out what problems each village faced. Some were interested in the trade union side and helped to explain, organise, and work with the labourers on the farms.

A spark was lit. One realised how just a small start somewhere, but with a concrete programme of work among the people, can inspire so much enthusiasm and hard work in such different sections of society. So many people—students, intellectuals, office workers, high-salaried executives, journalists and doctors came forward to help. And to learn, to change themselves in the process of changing, or trying to change, the miserable life of the toilers of Mehrauli.

What attracted people, I think, was that this was neither 'established' trade union work nor 'established' social work; the first with its overtones of corruption, vested interests, bureaucratic leadership only interested in the worker as long as he was on the shop floor, for his dues and as a political factor. Social work too was almost a dirty word, conjuring up images of painted ladies in silks and chiffons, raising funds at various balls and fetes to dole out here and there in charity. Alienated and alien, they created more dependence, more of the *mai-baap* mentality which had paralysed our people for so long.

With Paolo Freire in mind, we wanted to engage the people at every step in their own struggle for improvement. Nothing would be done *for* them. We would, at the start, certainly do everything *with* them, but eventually they must learn to do it for themselves, relying on their own unity, organisation, and effort. Today they could not speak for themselves. Our task was to help them learn to find their voice.

We believed that our work would be appreciated not only by the government, committed as it was to "socialism, secularism and democracy", but also by the gentry on the farms. These people were all civilised, highly educated pillars of our society. Not all of them were VIPs', but all of them were part of the modern, western-educated elite, and we were sure they would be responsive once they understood our work. How misplaced our confidence was, in fact, came as something of a shock at

first. Then it aroused anger and indignation, sharpening our
determination to fight on and to expose the hollow sham of our
'cherries on the cream'.

It was slow going. For several months we concentrated only
on instilling some confidence and awareness in the workers.
Every day there was a meeting on one farm or another. The
scheduled time was 9 p.m. after work and meals had been completed. Those of us who were city-bred and had a sense of time
would present ourselves on the dot only to find our host for the
night quite alone, peacefully smoking a *bidi*, finishing off his
meal, or fast asleep.

"Don't you remember the meeting?" we would ask.

"Of course, *Behnji*, I'll go and call them now." He would
rush off, and his voice would ring into the night, *"Aa jao, aa
jao, Behnji aa gayee!"* Then they would trickle in and by midnight we would be off to a swinging start. Meeting? It was so
hard to remember. A *kirtan*, yes, a *tamasha* of any kind, oh
yes, but meetings? This strange phenomenon took some getting
used to.

We would form a circle on the grass under the stars, and each
one would tell his name, where he came from, why he had come,
what his situation here was like. . . .Some of them could not
bring out the words. Consumed with shyness, dumb for centuries in the presence of *sahibs* like us, what could they say? But
with time and patience and persistence they would come out
with it one by one. Then we would compare notes, draw out
the similarities and differences in each one's tale and draw conclusions for the common interest.

It was the same story, whether from Rae Bareily, Pratapgarh,
Gonda, Sultanpur, Faizabad or Unnao. Landlessness, debt,
bonded labour, escape to the city, a desperate hand-to-mouth
subsistence here as well as there; voices cracked, eyes dull,
hearts dead.

But as we talked and talked, an interest was awakened—in
some sooner than in others, and it was these few who, once
inspired, began to take up the task of spreading the word among
their fellows. They persuaded them to come to meetings, to
think for themselves, to open up their minds and eyes. One of
these said to me, *"Behnji*, we are like sleeping men. You have
come and pricked a needle in our ears. It disturbs us, we shake

our heads and go back to sleep again. You must prick our ears with your needle again and again, and finally we will awaken."

Another said, "*Behnji*, we are like blind men groping for a way. If you can show us the path we will follow you—*anywhere!*"

"Why," I would tell them, "*Behnji* might lead you to a well— beware you don't jump in! No, my brothers, you must not take *Behnji*'s word blindly. You must weigh each thing, each step for yourselves. Think, is this for *our* good? Is this really in *our* interest? What do you know about *Behnji*? She lives in a big house and drives a car; she can betray you any time, run away, leave you. You must judge her too; at every step you must see whether she is with you, and the *extent* to which she is with you can only be known with time and experience. Take nothing on trust or blindly. Your friends are those who share your lives and struggle and no one else can be relied on."

This was our constant, conscious exhortation. It took a long while to penetrate, but we never lost sight of it, and finally they grasped it too. We must stand on our own feet, they began to understand. Fight our own fight, depend on our own strength. Those who come from outside, no matter who they are, are welcome as long as we keep the steering wheel in our own hands —once, that is, we have learned to drive, of course. This was the fundamental objective.

We were, in fact, as inexperienced as they were in the actual doing. The only difference was that we, free from oppression, and well read at least, were impelled by common sense and sheer natural justice. We knew nothing about the law, or about how to organise and what procedures to follow, but we too learned the slow and painful way. Above all we learned from the people—from their suffering, endurance, fear, and from their strength, their wisdom and their knowledge.

At last we were ready for our first step. The Registrar of Trade Unions, who was also a senior labour inspector, gave me details of the laws applicable to farm labour. The Minimum Wages Act of October 1971 held that the minimum wage for an eight hour day was, at that time, Rs 122 per month, with a weekly day of rest, twenty seven days annual leave, three gazetted holidays in the year and an overtime rate of double the normal wages for work done in excess of eight hours. A month's notice or pay in lieu was to be given for dismissal and, in the case of permanent workers (those who had worked for six months continuously were reckoned confirmed in their jobs or 'permanent'), a written charge sheet of offences had to be proved.

Minimal though it was, to us it seemed grand. The existing situation was that no one earned more than Rs 120 for a round-the-clock duty as *mali, chowkidar,* delivery boy and manager all rolled into one. Most workers were paid between eighty and ninety rupees a month. There was no question of any of them being given notice before dismissal, overtime rates or arrears of any kind. If someone came along and offered to do for eighty rupees what the present worker was doing for eighty five (and with a huge pool of unemployed this was frequent), the employer would unhesitatingly fire the one and hire the other.

It was a totally lawless situation, so when we finally plucked up enough courage to face the *maliks* we could begin almost anywhere. One of our first problems was that over 90% of the employers were absentee landlords and their ignorant, illiterate workers did not even know their full names, let alone their proper addresses. So we decided to start with those few who actually lived in their farms. Their treatment of the workers was usually much worse anyway, the absentee landlord at least being at a merciful distance most of the time.

Sardar Harnam Singh had a poultry farm. His workers were forcibly confined within this farm, made to work round the clock with only a couple of hours off for food and rest. They were abused and even beaten often, and now one of them had been fired without any settlement of account or wages due. The workers had had enough. A small band of about twenty men, comprising the fired hand's mates and other workers from neighbouring farms, assembled at the Sardarji's gate one morning and asked to see the *sahib.* He came out looking a bit surprised and apprehensive. When he heard what they had come for his face turned red.

"How dare you come here—be off! I'll not have this!"

The men held their ground and seeing one or two 'educated' people with them he appealed to us: "Please, won't you come in and sit down, I don't understand ... perhaps you can explain. ..."

But none of us moved. We explained that unless he asked all of us in we would prefer to talk to him out there. He got angry again. Then the men began to shout slogans. At this he quickly calmed down and began to offer terms. The dismissed man would be allowed to return if he wished, or if he preferred to leave he would be paid his dues in full. The Sardarji had not heard of any laws so far in this regard. We should understand that, and so on.

There was much jubilation after this. A victory had been won, a small demonstration of unity and determination had paid off. We could do it. We *can* do it!

The next case was that of Munnilal. Munnilal had worked as a tractor driver-cum-*mali* on the farm of the dreaded *Kali Mem* or Black Lady as she was popularly called. She had promised him a wage of Rs 180 per month, the job of driver being a skilled one. He had worked with her for a year and a half but except for one or two 'advances', he had not been paid a penny so far. He had made an arrangement to eat at a nearby tea shop and the shopkeeper, a villager from Sultanpur who knew that Munnilal was properly employed, had fed him all this time on credit. Now, in a fit of rage, the *Kali Mem* (wife of a ministerial secretary) had kicked Munnilal out. She had thrown his *teena* or tin of *atta* and oil outside the gate, put a lock on his quarter, literally ripped off the old pair of trousers and shirt she had given him to wear, and here he was, shivering in his underpants at our door. Indignation ran high and some five or six of us decided to go and investigate.

We arrived at the farm at about 5 p.m. and knocked at the big gate. The *Kali Mem* herself received us. She invited us in but we said that we had only come to find out what all this concerning Munnilal was about. We informed her of the laws in operation and she, swearing that she didn't owe Munnilal a penny, invited us back next morning when she would show us the written account of his work with her. We parted on that, perfectly friendly.

Imagine my surprise when, a few hours later, a villager from Sultanpur came running to the house.

"*Behnji*, you must do something quickly. The *Kali Mem* has come raging to the *Pradhan*. She says that a gang of 15 to 20 drunken men led by a *badmash si larki* had invaded her farm and created a riot. The *Pradhan* said yes, he knew all about those criminal *purabias* and their new 'saviour', and that he would take her at once to report the matter to the police. They have gone off now. Oh *Behnji*, what will happen?"

I calmed him down, but I was angry. The *Pradhan* of Sultanpur of course disliked us because of our attempt to start a night school for the harijans of his village, but that was no reason for him to go to these lengths.

"Come on," I said, "let's go at once to the police station ourselves. How dare they make such false reports?"

We set off. At the Mehrauli police station we met the SHO. We asked him if any complaint had been lodged by the lady and the *Pradhan* of Sultanpur. He said yes, such a complaint had been made. We rushed to Lado Sarai, a village just next to Mehrauli where the local Congress MLC, Prem Singh, lived. He was a harijan himself and had encouraged us when we had formed the Dehat Mazdoor Sudhar Sabha. He heard us out and rang the SHO. What was all this nonsense, he wanted to know, and asked the SHO not to do anything silly.

"It's all right," he said, putting the receiver down. "Don't you worry. You are doing good work, keep it up."

But the *Kali Mem* kept it up too. One day when I had gone to check some land records at the *tehsildar's* office which was just next to the police station, I saw her sitting with the SHO and a portly man who turned out to be her husband. When they saw me, the husband said, "I know all about you. You are here to make trouble because you are a Chinese agent. The Chinese pay you for this."

I was stunned, then furious. I demanded that the SHO take this down in writing. I wanted to make a complaint about these people.

"What complaint do you want to make? He didn't say anything," the SHO tried to laugh it off.

"You heard what he said," I told him, "kindly take down my complaint."

"I heard nothing," the SHO said smoothly.

That evening I had a visit from the *Kali Mem's* husband.

"You are an intelligent and educated person," he said. "My wife actually has great admiration for your guts. But these people you are trying to help, they are all rogues and thieves, you don't know them. They are criminals and a person like you should not get mixed up with them."

He was trying the old school tie bit with me. I told him that any settlement could only be made in front of all the people concerned and suggested our village headquarters in Sultanpur as a meeting place. On his way back his car was surrounded by angry villagers near Sultanpur, who demanded that he pay Munnilal the money owed him and apologise to me for his insulting remarks at the police station and for his wife's false reports as well. He promised to come back next morning and settle the matter.

Next day a large crowd gathered in the harijan *panchayat* house in Sultanpur. The *Kali Mem's* husband turned up on the dot of the appointed time. He apologised for his wife's behaviour and agreed to pay the entire sum claimed by Munnilal. But he insisted that the latter was claiming much more than was really his due.

"Madam, you don't believe me, but this lad has only worked for us for nine months and not the year and a half he is claiming."

We decided to investigate further and take from him only what was due. After a full investigation it turned out that Munnilal had indeed lied to us. He had exaggerated both his claim and the length of time he had worked on the farm. In our enthusiasm for the underdog we had overlooked the necessity for a proper check into the veracity of the claims brought forward. This could lead to serious problems. Not only the dishonesty of over-claiming, which for the impoverished is hardly surprising or a crime, but much more for the wrong tendencies this kind of thing would engender—opportunism, unfair and dishonest claims and unscrupulous exploitation of our hard-won unity. There was enough real injustice, real exploitation and real illegality; where was the need to fabricate? Our people must learn to fight for a *just* cause. Work hard and fight for your rights, I told them. We would get nowhere with shirking and opportunism.

A meeting was called in every *toli* and all this was explained carefully and seriously. The people understood. They did not *need* to put up false cases, their situation was bad enough as it was. Munnilal's deception was roundly condemned. He had dishonoured our union. This was a blow to our unity and our prestige. Munnilal had deceived his own brothers, which was the worst thing possible. But he thought we were fools. Unrepentant, he felt that we should take whatever we could grab. These people had cheated him, hadn't they? Why should we not cheat them in turn? He could not understand.

It was then decided that we must never again take up any case without proper investigation. This would mean hearing the worker's version, then checking his story with his fellow workers and their neighbours, and also anyone from the nearest village who might know something about the case. The villagers were held to be more reliable than the fly-by-night *purabias*. Then, on the basis of a carefully checked report, we would write to the employer concerned and inform him of the case received by the Union, asking for his side of the story before we took it up as a Union matter. This became a basic mode of procedure. Munnilal had taught us a lesson. We would not take up any false cases. We must establish ourselves as honest, incorruptible, and fair, but once we were certain that a case was correct, we would fight with all the strength at our command to win the rights of the worker concerned.

By unanimous decision Munnilal's case was dropped. This was in fact a sign of the Union's weakness at the time. We should at least have got him paid for the work he had done. But his unrepentant attitude about his dishonesty and the harm it did to our reputation was too much for the workers to stomach. They did not have the heart to face the *Kali Mem* again. All the same it had taught us all some valuable lessons. Firstly, it once again confirmed the strength that lay in unity—even the fierce *Kali Mem* had been successfully confronted. Secondly, it taught us from the city not to be naive and over-enthusiastic, not to romanticise the poor. We had to recognise their weaknesses, their selfishness and opportunism. We had to guard against these tendencies and help the workers to overcome them. They would have to develop confidence based on the justice of their cause, not on the ability to cheat.

Thus were the foundations of our union laid. It was a slow,

step-by-step process and the pitfalls were many. But each stage
was discussed collectively, analysed minutely. We tried to draw
correct lessons from each experience so that we could learn
from our mistakes and go forward more surely.

The Dehat Mazdoor Union was registered in February 1973. It
was a moment of triumph. We had come a long way from our
beginnings, but we knew only too well we had a long, long way
to go before we could reach our goal—the recognition of our
human dignity after centuries of degraded existence.

Our first step after registration was to prepare a cyclostyled
notice to the farm owners informing them of the terms of the
Minimum Wages Act as applicable to farm labour. We suggested holding a meeting with them either at our office in Sultanpur
or in the office of the Labour Commissioner (which is what the
latter had suggested), or some other mutually convenient place.
We made it clear that we realised that agriculture was not a
cut-and-dried business, and that the terms of the Act could be
modified to suit both parties if an agreement was reached. Not
a single employer replied to our notice or even acknowledged
its receipt.

We waited for about three months and then decided to take
up cases as they arose. Any more inaction would have frustrated
the enthusiasm of the workers who were looking forward to the
implementation of their rights.

We had been told by the Labour Commissioner's office that
the method of taking up a case was to send a letter to
the employer bringing to his notice the complaint of his
employee and requesting either direct remedial action or
a reply within seven days of receiving our letter. If neither was
done, we were to give notice that we would meet the employer
personally at his farm or in our office on a given date and time.
Copies of all correspondence were to be sent to the Labour
Commissioner.

Our Union of course was extremely poor. With an average
wage of about a hundred rupees per month, the annual fee for
the Union was fixed at four rupees with a one rupee membership
fee. To collect even this proved difficult, and we had to
take it in instalments as no one could pay the full five rupees

at once. So in the matter of correspondence with the employers we had to economise as indeed we had to in everything else as well. We began by getting each worker to deliver the Union's letter to his *malik* by hand. These were summarily refused. We then got a member of the Executive Committee of the Union, armed with an official messenger's book, to deliver our notices and letters and to get the *malik's* signature on receipt. This method was also rejected by the employers. They would either not accept the letter at all or, if they did, they would refuse to sign the book and afterwards pretend ignorance of any communication at all.

We had to take recourse to the postal service in the end, and tried mailing our letters by ordinary post. But the *maliks* insisted that no letter had ever reached them, and so finally we were forced to expend our slender resources on sending each letter by Registered Acknowledgement Post, if only to have proof that the letters had been delivered. Each such letter sent cost Rs 1.50 or thereabouts, so that in each case almost three of the annual four rupees fee were spent on merely letting the *malik* and the labour court know that such and such worker had brought such and such complaint against his employer to the notice of the Union.

This was clearly beyond our means, but no one, neither the employers nor the labour court, neither the police nor the administration, ever took this into account. What was stark reality for us was for them only a matter of 'rules'. If we wanted to form a Union we must follow the prescribed procedures and that was that.

Since the labour court was located in Rajpur Road some twenty miles away in Old Delhi, and with the limitations of the public transport system, each trip to the Labour Court took up a whole day. Often, when bus after overfull bus passed without stopping for us, we were obliged to take a scooter-rickshaw or motorcycle four-seater in order to be on time. It was easy to incur an expense of two or three rupees per person with fares and some small refreshment like a cup of tea in the course of a long day. Common sense soon put an end to this absurd situation and we decided to take to direct action on the farms instead. Registered letters, however, were still sent to the employers informing them of our wish to meet them at their farms at an appointed time, as we had been warned that we could be held for trespass otherwise.

The *maliks* usually descended on their farms (those who lived or happened to be in Delhi) at weekends, for picnics, swimming parties, booze-ups and related orgies. Their embarrassment can be imagined when, in the middle of their frolics with their friends, a band of ragged *purabias* appeared at their gates demanding an interview. A hostile response would lead to slogans and speeches exposing the shameful exploitation of the *malik*, and the red-faced host would quickly climb down. He would try asking us 'educated' ones in, pulling out chairs and offering us refreshments. But these items were always refused unless they applied to all present. And then he had to give us a hearing.

Of course he would reject our claims out of hand as a first response; this was pure reflex. Then would begin a ding-dong battle. The *malik* would lose patience with these ignorant wretches who had the insolence to raise the question of their 'rights' with their masters. Rights? They had never heard such cheek! This was the work of communists, naxalites, bad characters and trouble makers who had come here to disturb the peace. The police would be called and would arrive within minutes. Eject this scoundrel, throw out his belongings, I don't want to see him on my farm again, the *malik* would demand. The police, ever at the *maliks* service, would shout and swear and wield their *lathis* and, if they caught the unfortunate worker alone, they would evict him physically from his hut, throw out his belongings and send him packing with the warning that he would be arrested if he showed his face again.

Terror gripped the *maliks* at first, and we ourselves were nonplussed by this development. Then we were told that the police had no right to intervene in a dispute between an employer and his employees unless law and order were threatened. We also found out that it was illegal to evict a tenant without a court order. The problem now, however, was to overcome the fear in the people of the police. The *lal-topi* or red-capped policeman was a dreaded spectre in the lives of these people. Whether back in their villages or here in their present day lives, he haunted them—extorting bribes, threatening violence, fabricating charges, abusing and harassing

them at every turn. The poor and illiterate had no defence
against the daily violation of legality perpetrated on them
by the police, and it took a lot of effort and struggle before they
were able to overcome their fear and challenge the police
at their game. Until this happened they were beaten every time.
The biggest setback we experienced involved the case of a
worker who was employed on the stud farm belonging to a
general.

The general lived in a palatial mansion on his ninety acre
stud and agricultural farm, breeding thoroughbred race horses
for export. The farm, a showpiece in the area, was a model of
modern, efficient and immaculate upkeep. The condition
of the farmhands however, was not so immaculate. We were
told that although the *syces* had an 18 hour day not a single
one was paid more than Rs 110 per month, and this for
the senior hands some of whom had been working there for
over ten years. Their living quarters had no latrines, and if anyone was caught defecating on the ninety acre premises he was
fined two rupees. The fine for urinating was one rupee and
anyone caught eating a carrot meant for the horses was
fined five rupees. If a worker fell sick or had to take a day off
his wages for that day were cut. There were no off-days and
no leave of any kind by right. Physical assault by the management was not infrequent as also were injuries from the high-
spirited horses. If any worker was injured so seriously that
he was useless for further work he was thrown out with
no compensation and replaced with one of the army of always
available unemployed. All this was told to us not only by
the workers but by some men in the lower management as well.

Some time back, before our Union had been formed, we had
had a stark example of the general's inhumanity to his work
force. One of his farmhands had come to us for medical help
with his wife and small baby. All three were suffering from
acute malnutrition. The woman had actually lost her reason
and was beyond help. The baby was in a horrible condition.
They said he was two years old but he looked no more than six
months. Hideously deformed by malnourishment, he was a
mere skeleton with a huge head, great bulging eyes and quite
motionless. They had already lost their firstborn the same way
and the mother had gone mad with grief. We could do nothing

of course, but we offered to take the child to the hospital at once. The father was hesitant; he thought it would mean expense and he only earned Rs 90 a month. We explained that it was a government hospital and would cost him nothing.

The doctors in the emergency ward took one look at the child and exclaimed in horror that it was in an extreme stage of malnutrition. "You should have come months ago," they told us. Seeing that there was an 'educated' person with the family, they were very helpful and admitted the child into hospital at once and fought hard to save its life. The baby died on the seventh day.

It was a hospital rule that a relative should arrange to stay in with the patient to look after his everyday needs, the hospital staff being too rushed to do this themselves. As the child's mother was mentally unsound his father had to take leave to stay with him. When he returned to work he was told that seven days wages would be cut for the days he had absented himself from work.

After the Union was formed, there was another case on the general's farm. Kedar Nath was a young Nepali. Intelligent and literate, he wrote songs and poetry for the Union and was a merry, sweet-natured and hard-working young man. He became a good friend and we used to meet often and explain to him how to organise the workers on the stud farm. Then he disappeared. We did not seen him for weeks and wondered what had happened to him. He was, at that time, our only contact on the stud farm.

One day I saw an ashen-faced, bald-headed old man staggering through Gadaipur village. He sat down on the root of a tree and waited till I passed, greeting me then with a vacant smile and in a quavering voice.

"Don't you recognise me? I am Kedar Nath," he said.

Stunned, I tried to find out from him what had happened. He couldn't tell me much, his voice kept wandering and getting faint. Several people had gathered round and one of them now told me what had happened.

It seemed that Kedar Nath had taken out one of the horses for exercise. The horse was in a wicked mood and it had suddenly kicked out and knocked him over. Then it kicked viciously at his head and shoulders and he was finally dragged away unconscious by his mates and rushed to hospital. After two days on the danger list he pulled through and some weeks later he was discharged. But he could neither walk nor see nor hear properly. His left thumb had been amputated and he was a physical and to some extent mental wreck. We were told that the general had let him stay on in his quarter but without pay. The wages due to him before the accident had been cut to make up for his absence in hospital.

This was too much even for his cowed-down fellow mates. They all loved Kedar and they had had their fill of oppression. Now they wanted action. They were ready for anything, they told us; just give them the word.

We told them that this was a serious case and we would need to consult a lawyer and find out what could be done for Kedar. Meanwhile they must strengthen their unity and prepare for a hard struggle to end this injustice, but they must not take any action, we warned, until we had consulted a lawyer.

We went to the Labour Court, talked with a lawyer friend and came back armed with a watertight case. The stud farm was a profit-making industry and as such came under the Industrial Disputes Act as well as the Delhi Shops and Establishments Act and the Workmen's Compensation Act. We could demand not only a full settlement for Kedar Nath, but a thoroughgoing change in the conditions of employment as a whole.

We sent a letter to the general informing him of these laws and making some fourteen demands including medical treatment and financial compensation for Kedar, the abolition of fines and the establishment of proper facilities, emoluments and terms of service under the various laws applicable.

The general did not reply to us but he sent for his head *syce* who was dealt a blow and told that he was the ring leader in all this and no more nonsense would be tolerated from him. The rest of the workers downed tools and walked off in protest, and the general lost his nerve. His horses were shortly going to be sent off to Bombay, and a single day's neglect could affect their peak condition and ruin his huge profits. He hurriedly called all the workers together and, speaking to them "like a father", told them that they should bring their troubles to him instead of resorting to silly things like the Union. He would raise their wages by Rs 10 per head, but all the other demands were sheer mischief. He told them to come back to work; he looked upon them as his own children and would see that their difficulties were solved.

Unused to such tones, the workers were disarmed and agreed to resume work. But they soon realised that they had been duped and came running to the Union. We told them how they had lost a real chance to press home their advantage. But at least they could see how much the general feared their unified action. Now they must reject his settlement and demand that all fourteen points in the letter the Union had sent him be fulfilled. These were their minimum legal rights, no more.

Heady nights of meetings, earnest discussions, and careful guard against the omnipresent *chamchas*, culminated at last in a decision that all sixty workers on the farm would march to the general's house, supported by a contingent of the workers from other farms, and insist on a reply to their letter of demands. If they got no satisfaction they would declare a strike. If timed now, the strike would throw the general into a panic because there were only six weeks left before his horses were due to be sent to Bombay.

The general was informed of the proposed plan. He quickly swung into action. He threatened his men that if they struck work he would call in the army to evict them and take over the horses themselves. Although he was retired now he had been a senior officer in the army and this was no idle threat. He also called in the police on the day of the proposed march. They arrived in force early that morning, and the SHO, Mokhum Singh, came in a wireless-equipped jeep. They forbade the workers, on pain of arresting them, to have anything to do with the march.

When the rest of us, consisting of some fifty workers from other farms and myself, reached the gates of the general's farm, where his men were supposed to join us, we found them going about their work as usual, not one of them so much as daring to glance our way, and SHO Mokhum Singh standing by his jeep looking very bland.

We had proposed no trespass, no violence, no illegality; only a meeting with the general to discuss our fourteen demands and negotiate a settlement. But his strong-arm reaction had broken his workers' nerve and, just as we had warned them he would do if they lost heart halfway through, he waited till his horses

were safely away and then sacked every last man of them. They
were told to leave without notice, without wages and with no
accounts settled. Their unity, morale and courage shattered,
they did just that. It was a bitter defeat. This was the only farm
on which there were enough hands to be able to make a show
of force, but they had proved unequal to the task and lost what
they could so easily have won with the law so unambiguously
on their side.

But every defeat taught us valuable lessons. This one made
us realise that we had been taken in by the enthusiasm of the
stud farm workers when in fact they had not been sufficiently
tried in struggle to be able to withstand the very first assault
from the general. Strength and determination did not come from
enthusiasm alone, but would have to be won gradually and with
great patience and restraint.

The terrorisation of the workers by the police was illegal and
had to be challenged. But it was difficult to find a worker who
was strong enough to stand firm and refuse to be cowed by the
appearance of the police and the threats they made in order to
force his surrender to his *malik's* demands.

Then the case of Ram Phal came up. Ram Phal was a proud
and self-respecting man. He worked as a *mali, chowkidar* and
dairyman on the farm of a highly educated professional couple.
He was also the vice-president of the Dehat Mazdoor Sudhar
Sabha which had been organised before the Union was formed.
Ram Phal had worked for four years on this farm and was paid a
monthly wage of a hundred rupees as *mali* and watchman. Over
the past year or so his employers had started a mini-dairy, keeping a cow or two as well, and they had promised Ram Phal an
extra two rupees a day for looking after the cows. So far he had
not received a penny of that money. He, his family, and the
cows lived together in a thatched shack. One day while he was
milking the cows the fire that had been lit to keep the mosquitoes
away was accidentally kicked over and set the thatching alight.
Ram Phal managed to save the cows, his wife and children, but
the thatched roof burned down and he lost all his bedding and
clothes in the blaze. The mistress of the farm, whose vitriolic
tongue had already inflicted many wounds on Ram Phal's pride,

now arrived in a fury, accused him of arson and ordered him off her farm at once. Ram Phal, who was slow to anger but stubborn once aroused, dug his heels in and refused to move until she had paid him his promised dues. He told her that he had no wish to remain in her employ as he had had enough of her abusive tongue, but he would not go until she paid him for the work he had done all year with the cows. He also demanded that he be paid according to the provisions of the Minimum Wages Act for all his other work as well. This amounted to several thousand rupees and according to the law he had a right to every penny of it.

Then the Union sent a notice to Ram Phal's employers informing them of the provisions of the law and referring them to the Labour Court if they wanted confirmation. The notice infuriated the mistress of the farm. Confusing the Labour Court with a 'People's Court', she spread the story that we were threatening to hold a people's court on her farm and that she and her husband were in danger of their lives. She accused us of taking the law into our own hands and swore to get even with us and "have us brought to our senses" before long.

To police were called in and ordered to throw Ram Phal and his family off the farm. But Ram Phal stood firm and the Union stood firm behind him. We challenged the police, led as usual by the egregious Mokhum Singh, to go ahead and break, once again, the laws they were supposed to protect. They backed down and after a long hassle Ram Phal was paid the amount we were demanding. This in the end was only a computation of the two rupees a day he was due for tending the cows. We overlooked all the other claims as these would have run into thousands. We did this after full consultation among ourselves because this was a test case, and also because we knew that these employers, despite their autocratic behaviour, were in fact people of modest means. Their attitude was their own worst enemy, however, and the workers were reluctant to let them off at the outset. Instead of acting according to their much proclaimed democratic pretensions they behaved no better than any feudal lord, and gave in at last only because they realised that they could not move us and that if we wanted we could claim the entire amount they in fact owed Ram Phal. They tried to bargain with us, saying that if Ram Phal would only vacate the farm premises they would pay up all that the court instructed. But the labour officer had told us that as long as a dispute was pending there was no question of eviction.

Moreover, we had had bitter experience in the past of agreeing to move off the premises, usually because of the weakness of the employee involved, only for the *malik* blandly to deny all knowledge of the man. Nor had we any proof, in the absence of any letter of appointment or record of wages (both of which were legally required but never complied with), that a worker was actually employed on a particular farm. There was nothing we could do in such cases except lay a long siege on the employer. We had to keep off his farm, however, or else we could be charged with trespass, and it was well nigh impossible, given the scattered state of the *purabias* in ones and twos on a farm, to get them together in time to waylay the *malik* on one of his infrequent visits to his farm.

So Ram Phal won his case and was the hero of the hour. He had stood firm. And because he had stood firm his supporters in the Union had stood firm too. Each victory had its lessons as well. If a worker could just hang on long enough his *malik*, faced with constant pressure, would finally give in, pay up what was demanded under the law—or rather what we were able finally to negotiate on that basis—and thankfully see the last of us for a while.

This process went on for almost a year. Victory after victory led to an increased consciousness in the farm workers of their strength in unity. The connection between the strength and persistence of the worker or workers directly concerned in a case and that of their supporters in the Union was gradually realised. It was a vital link because the rest of the labour force could be accused of trespass, illegal interference etc., if those on the spot climbed down or were browbeaten into submission by their *maliks*. But if they held out then the support of their fellow workers from neighbouring farms invariably led to victory.

The *maliks* reacted as one. It was a revelation of the elite of our country to witness their reaction to the mere suggestion that they implement the minimum labour legislation on their farms. They reacted to the very idea that their employees had any such thing as rights. Their attitude was that these *purabias* had never raised their heads let alone their voices all these years, and now this rabble-rousing, no-good naxalite, CIA agent Primila Lewis had come and turned the place upside down. Rights? Legal rights or any rights at all? The bloody nerve! Crush them now other-wise we won't be able to stop them—this was the unanimous opinion. There was no hint in any one of them of the remotest democratic consciousness, and yet these were our most 'modern' gentry. It was a shocking disappointment to realise how thin was the veneer of our democracy.

As soon as an employee presented his claim or the Union sent a letter to the *malik*, the wheels went into action. First the worker would be threatened with jail or worse if he did not leave the premises at once. If threats failed, they would send *goondas* or the police, although the latter had to move more cautiously now. Those who succumbed at this stage were forced to sign or, as most of them were illiterate, to put a thumbprint on a blank sheet of paper or under a notice saying that all their accounts had been settled and they were leaving the farm of their own accord. Where these tactics failed as well, we won.

It took a lot of courage to stand up to these threats and this intimidation from the combined might of the Indian elite and its police-cum-*goonda* force. Facing them was the *purabia bhayya*, gentle, simple, illiterate, timid, and often terrified, but goaded on by a glimmer of new light, hope, and understanding.

Victory after victory breathed new life into the Union. Its ranks expanded and new *tolis* sprang up in every area. The vil-lagers, some disconcerted, some hostile some encouraging, but all impressed—"*Purabion men jaan aa gayi!*" ("The Purabias have come to life")—looked on with increasing interest. Stone workers, quarry workers, brick workers, oppressed by their *sardars* and *jamadars* and contractors, took note. The workers in the factories which had sprung up in some of the villages began to stir. The village youth came forward. They wanted to start *yuva sabhas* in their villages and they wanted the Union to help them. The morale of the *purabias* was high. "Our" Union—it really was *ours*.

New rules were laid down: attendance at *toli* meetings and assistance in each other's cases became a precondition for taking on a new case. Domestic quarrels, caste, village or district rivalries, 'woman' problems, kidnapping, drunkenness, and especially the intake of *bhang* or marijuana, all came under the scrutiny of the Union now. A new confidence and pride was articulated—*we can refashion our lives, we can change the world!*

New problems came to light all the time and were tackled with enthusiasm. Despite spiralling prices and shortages of the most essential commodities even in the black market, this huge number of immigrant workers (the overall total was in tens of thousands) was without ration cards. Since the *maliks* could not be bothered to procure them for their farm workers, those few who had ventured to the ration authorities for help had been informed, after days of standing in a queue, that immigrant workers could only be issued cards if they were able to produce a written affidavit from the *pradhan* back in their home village to the effect that they held no cards there. Then they had also to produce an affidavit from the *pradhan* of the village under whose jurisdiction they now resided, from the local MLC and from their employer as well, confirming that they held no cards here either in case they might be concealing them to get more rations. If they could produce all these, they would be issued a temporary ration card for three months, which is all they were entitled to as immigrants, and thereby designated 'homeless'. Some who had tried this procedure had had no response from the first source (the *pradhan* of their village of origin) even after two or three years. But most had not even made the effort, knowing the futility of it. *Pradhans* and MLCs' were big people, not concerned with the needs of these *purabias*.

The Union decided to take up the matter. The General Secretary and two or three other committee members went to the circle ration office in Sarvodaya Enclave, some five miles away. They were told to go away, and even application forms were refused them since it seemed there were 'orders' that no ration cards were to be given to immigrant workers. Next day we took a small procession of some fifty workers to the ration office and raised slogans demanding ration cards. We were handed a heap of application forms, told that they had run out of more, and promised that we could have as many as were needed as soon as their supplies were replenished. We then checked with the Commissioner for Food and Supplies who told us that not only was every man, woman and child, no matter what their status, entitled to a ration card, but that he was grateful to us for trying to achieve this in our area. He said that there was an unholy alliance between the ration inspectors, fair price shops and the black market, all of whom profiteered on the thousands of 'ghost' ration cards which properly belonged to the migrant labourers of Delhi but had been siphoned off instead into the black market. The ignorant labourers could be easily deceived and browbeaten, and if we could help to curb these activities he would be very happy.

The applications, duly completed, were reluctantly accepted by the ration officers who prevaricated over giving any dates for delivery of the cards. The *purabias*, unable to buy grain at the prohibitive black market prices, were desperate. They organised another demonstration. This time over four hundred workers marched to the ration office, cheered on by people in the streets and town of Mehrauli. The demonstration created panic at the ration office. Armed police were rushed to the spot. The anti-government movement in Gujarat had exploded, the food situation was serious, and Delhi did not want food riots at its door. We blocked the entry to and exit from the ration office, and told the people waiting in line that we would see that they got their work done first, but today they should support us as they too were harassed by the ration authorities. They were only too ready to join us, most of them were poor and had been coming here day after day without result. A middle-class Tamilian family living on the first floor above the ration office told us that the government, which had rented their ground floor, had not paid them any rent for months, and they asked us to do something about that too. The police formed a cordon and begged us not to try and break our way into the office. The SDM arrived, and then the Regional Commissioner for Food and Supplies. Until now the ration officers had insisted that they could do nothing, it would take time, etc., etc. We had said we could wait but were not going back until we got our cards.

The Regional Commissioner was sympathetic and reprimanded his subordinates. He told them to get down to some hard work for once in their lives, and ordered them to start processing the cards at once. We offered to help and began checking entries, and filling up forms along with the office staff. Our main demand was that from now on the stamp of Dehat Mazdoor Union over the signature of the president or general secretary should be sufficient as an affidavit for anyone needing a ration

card. This was conceded. The ration office staff scurried about
trying to organise itself. The clerks and officers worked well into
the night and every last man got his work done that day. We
marched back to the farms through the streets of Mehrauli,
shouting victorious slogans and full of joy at our triumph.

This incident had a major impact on the people. Not only the
farm workers but others too, similarly harassed day in and day
out by the petty bureaucracy, now saw that determination in a
just cause, unity, and struggle were the only way to combat such
harassment. Slum and *jhuggi* dwellers from all over south Delhi
now began to come to us. They also wanted to organise and
work with us. They wanted us to come to their colonies and
show them the way.

As the movement surged forward, those individuals in the
Union who at various stages had come forward, showing more
interest, understanding, courage and initiative than the others
(and from among whom the Union's Executive Committee had
been elected), now went to these areas and explained to their new
friends the long, hard, but only way to improvement and change.
Their constant theme was that they must not look for outside
leadership, outside help, and things for free. If they wanted
change, they must first change themselves, their own attitudes,
and learn to be independent.

I wish I could write about each one of those men—how,
slowly, the light dawned, consciousness was born, friendship
grew and was cemented in trust and common struggle; about the
jealousies and competitiveness too, and the selfish individualism
and egoism; and how, step by step, we battled against these
weaknesses and stumbling blocks. How patiently, collectively
in the *toli* meetings and individually as well, we gradually learned the vital lesson that mistakes and weaknesses are nothing
to be ashamed of as long as our effort is always directed towards
understanding the nature of such weaknesses and mistakes and
then trying to overcome them. How false pride, false prestige,
covering up, would only block and obstruct our way forward,
for we would not be able to bring about change if we placed our
personal, individual, selfish interests above those of the larger
collective interest and of society as a whole. Nor could
individual heroism, or the 'leadership *chakkar*' of ambition and
careerism bring about any real change.

The question of leadership was an important one for us. What is correct leadership? Who should lead? How are leaders made? Initially, and for a long time in fact, the idea among the workers was that leadership could only come from us *babus*, middle-class people from outside. It was only *pare-likhe log*—educated people —after all, who could show them the way. They themselves were too illiterate, ignorant and afraid to become leaders. This of course was partly true, or entirely true for a while—but only until they themselves learned the ropes, learned to "drive their own engine", as they used to say. The idea that the 'rabble' is not fit to do anything but follow where it is led has been nurtured for centuries, and it took the *purabias* some time to see through this ancient game. It took time to understand why and how the *babus* and their ilk, the professional politicians, 'leaders', social workers might have quite another set of interests from their own—that they might only want to use them for their own ends, deliberately keeping them in the dark about the 'dialectics of liberation'. The realisation came slowly that these *babus* must prove themselves in practice, and should not be taken on trust simply at face value, or for the speeches they made so easily. The principle—learn from everyone but rely on ourselves and test the others over time and in the course of struggle—was grasped by some earlier than others, but those who did finally grasp it would not let it go easily again.

The year 1973-74 was one of intense and varied experience, of consolidation and expansion. But the period of triumph, of riding high, did not last long beyond that. Bitter, painful struggles lay ahead, and the Union was to be put to severe tests in the attempts to crush it. But although it was badly shaken, it was never altogether crushed.

The farm workers realised after a while that to collect what seemed a large sum of money as their *hissab* or account, and then to leave the farm, was hardly a solution. Five hundred or a thousand rupees seemed a lot at first. With this, the worker could return to his village with new clothes for the family and money to pay a good part of the debt to the moneylender. But then what? Out of a job, with no prospects at home, he would have to come back to the city and begin the old round again, the hunt for work, any work to fill his stomach for the day. What was needed was job security, not just the pay off *hissabs*.

This was the next stage of the struggle. It was decided that the *maliks* had had ample time to come to terms with the law. Now they must be forced to implement it. The Labour Commissioner's office had told us that after six months of continuous work an employee became permanent on the roll, i.e., confirmed in his job. He could only be dismissed if a written charge sheet of offences was proved against him. We now decided to fight for the implementation of this aspect of the law. Our basic demand was for a minimum wage of Rs 170 per month for an eight-hour day, with responsibility for the farm—but not as a watchman— a weekly day off, and a month's annual leave. So far not a single employer had implemented these provisions, which were all included in the Minimum Wages Act. Indeed, any worker who demanded his rights the *maliks* attempted immediately to dismiss. A long and stubborn struggle usually lasting at least two months would finally result in the farm worker being paid his dues and dismissed from his job. Up to that point the worker had had to do without his wages, be subjected to all manner of threats and intimidation from the *malik*, his *goondas* and the police, and keep body and soul together with the support both material and moral of his fellow farm workers. These, be it noted, were half-starved themselves and often gave up their daily wages in order to be on the spot where a fellow worker was involved in a case.

This was clearly intolerable and unjust. The workers demanded that a strike be declared in the whole area. The winter wheat was ripening when the call "*Gehun Katai Bandh*" ("The Crop Will Not Be Cut"), was sent out to all the workers on the farms. The Executive Committee declared that the crop would not be cut until the employers met the demand for the fair implementation of the Minimum Wages Act, including job security for the workers. The employers would have to give in writing to each of their workers that he was employed on these terms and at the minimum wage computed at Rs 170 per month.

The decision to go on strike was a big step and would need a lot of courage and perseverance. Some of us, and especially Srilata and I (she had joined us some months earlier), were doubtful whether the men would be able to sustain such a strike in the face of the expected heavy-handed reaction of the VIP landlords. They had formed their own association by now, with the sole object of destroying the Union. The grapevine was buzzing with rumours of how they intended to go about it. There was no legal way and they wanted to provoke us into some illegal act. We heard that they were even contemplating physical violence on the 'leaders' to frighten us into leaving the area. My family and I had already been forced to leave our house in Gadaipur village, and now we were being continuously harassed in the house to which we had moved. The landlady was an especially virulent opponent of the Union, and had acted brutally and illegally to get rid of her own *mali* who had worked with her for four years and then been thrown out by the police without getting a penny of what was owed him. This woman had powerful connections in the government, her husband being a ministerial secretary.

But our main concern regarding the proposed strike was the uneven strength of the Union from area to area. Some *tolis* were strong and had been tested over time; they would be able to stand firm under pressure. But we doubted whether others, formed comparatively recently, would be able to withstand the first hint of repression. The Committee, however, was adamant.

"*Behnji*, we have put the question squarely before every *toli*, and the decision is unanimous," was the reply.

"It is up to you," we told them. "If you are ready then we are."

The plans were chalked out. A sub-committee was elected in each *toli* and made responsible for arranging for all eventualities. First it would call on the local strength, then on surrounding *tolis*, and finally, if needed, on the whole Union for a big case. Two committee members were on duty round the clock to be on call for the needs of every *toli*. A mobile squad of about fifty workers was formed which would move rapidly to every trouble spot. It was decided that if the *maliks* agreed to implement the law all would be well, otherwise the wheat would not be harvested. But it was also decided that the crop must not be allowed to rot. If necessary it would be cut and stored, and if the *maliks* still held out, the workers would use it themselves to feed on and sell in the market in order to sustain themselves while the strike lasted.

This was a bold step indeed. But the situation had reached a point where there seemed to be no other way to bring the arrogant gentry to its senses. The chagrin of the *maliks* can be imagined when they descended on their farms that spring of 1974 to oversee the cutting of the crop, only to be met with a solid wall of refusal. Their reaction, after the first expostulations was one of sweet reasonableness: "Okay, okay—here, take your hundred and seventy rupees for this month. We'll give you what you want if that is the law, don't worry. Now be good chaps and get on with the cutting. You don't want the crop to rot do you? What? You want us to give it to you in writing? Who ever heard of such a thing! You won't cut the crop unless we do? Can't you trust us? Have we ever deceived you? We are saying we'll give you your Rs 170, what more do you want? All right, we haven't the time just now, but next time we come we will give it to you in writing. Now get along and start cutting."

The simple *purabias*, thinking that all was won and the *sahibs* not so bad after all, set to work with a will. The crop was cut, bagged and stored. And then, when the Union's guard was down, the gentry descended again: "Look here, you thieving scoundrels," they said, "You will take your Rs 110, or 120, or 130 as before, or get out NOW. Rs 170 indeed! Act and laws indeed!"

With SHO Mokhum Singh and his police, or with their own 'bodyguards' in support, they came: the generals and industrialists, the diplomats and business executives, the politicians and their flunkeys—all played the same dirty trick. Mokhum Singh laughed. "Minimum Wages Act? There is no such thing. Labour Courts? Not for scum like you! Be off, or I'll arrest you for wilful trespass and beat the stuffing out of you."

Those that held out, sticking to their demands for job security and a hundred and seventy rupees per month, and refusing to budge from the premises whatever the threats and compulsions, were able to stay on. But it was a long, long struggle, with neither side giving in for months until finally a compromise was reached at a sum of money somewhere between what the workers were demanding and what the *malik* had been paying them before. But the strike had an electrifying effect, the gauntlet was down, and now the farm owners, fully exposed by the shameless violation of both their word and the law, were determined to fight it out to the finish.

The owners used all their influence, and this was considerable, to crush the Union. The police, the administration, the labour courts were powerless to carry out their ostensible duties. Initially a few of the more senior officials in these services had been sympathetic and helpful. But now, with the VIPs on the offensive, and with names like Gandhi and Nehru among them, what bureaucrat dared to challenge them? We were warned to cool things down or we would find ourselves in serious trouble. Yes, it was conceded, our demands were reasonable and our cause was just—but we had chosen the wrong area. Didn't we know? Mehrauli was the most corrupt spot in India! An SDM said: "Everyone knows that these people are flouting the law, but who can stop them? Who will bell the cat?"

The farm owners' favourite tactic now was to frame false charges against the workers and call in the police who were ever ready to come to their help. Workers were indiscriminately arrested on a variety of trumped-up charges, taken to the police station, beaten and tortured to extract 'confessions' and incriminate others, and then, unless bailed out, were put in jail.

The first reactions of terror soon gave way to indignation and resistance, and we decided to resist arrest unless proper warrants and charges were made. We also complained to the District Commissioner, V.K. Kapoor, about the illegal evictions and arrests of workers from the farms by the police, and he, being one of the rare honest and enlightened public servants in the field, was able to put a stop to these for a time. But he was soon transferred from his job. The man who became all powerful after this was the notorious Navin Chawla, then Additional District Magistrate for South Delhi (ADM), and a personal friend of Sanjay Gandhi. Navin Chawla was determined to prove his friendship and make good his career by, amongst other things, ridding the 'royal family' of us nuisances in Mehrauli.

For although the administration and police had turned against us on orders from above, the press and parliament now stepped in and, taking up the situation on the VIP farms in Mehrauli as something of a cause, made quite an issue about the way all these VIPs, including Mrs Gandhi, were violating the law. When

Walter Schwarz of *The Guardian* decided to visit the area as well, and there were prospects of the news getting out abroad, Navin Chawla had to resort to other ways of putting us down.

Some examples of the kind of cases fabricated against the workers should be given. Two workers were accused of stealing five acres of *bajra* in a single night and spiriting it away by morning. When the police were called they could find no trace of the stolen crop. But they established the exact time of the alleged theft, and the two *malis* were taken to the police station in Mehrauli where they were hung upside down and beaten on the soles of their feet to make them confess to the theft.

Not only were these third degree methods totally illegal, but our protests, and the fact that the two men had been attending a meeting from 8 p.m. to 12 midnight in their *toli*, during which time the theft was supposed to have occurred, made no difference. We had the register in which their names, as also the names of all those who attended the meeting that night were recorded, and the time when it started and ended was also entered, all in accordance with our normal procedure. But the police did not want any evidence contrary to that of the *malik's*.

Another example was that of Maya Ram, who worked on the farm of an extremely well-connected family. He was relatively new to the Union, but he had decided to join the strike. One evening the woman who employed him arrived on the farm with a posse of *goondas*. Maya Ram was alone; they locked him into the bathroom of their farm house, loaded on to a truck all the wheat which he had stored and was refusing to part with until he was paid according to the law, and drove off. I was told by no less a person than Navin Chawla himself, that the lady had then got on the phone to Mrs Gandhi, and complained to her about the scandalous situation on her farm where she had been forcibly locked into her own bathroom by a horde of *purabias* led by that dreadful Primila Lewis, who had refused to let her remove her crop. Mrs Gandhi, it seems, rang the Lt. Governor as head of the Delhi Administration, and told him to take suitable action on the situation in Mehrauli which he seemed to have allowed to get out of hand. The Lt. Governor, thus chastised, questioned Navin Chawla in turn, and the latter was determined to act decisively. For the unpardonable had happened; Mrs Gandhi's displeasure had been aroused.

The Himalaya Spun Pipe Factory in the village of Fatehpur Beri was owned by a Mr Aggarwal, who employed about eighty workers. Mr Aggarwal, like the rest of his kind in the area, observed none of the legal regulations which applied to his factory or to his workers, nor had they heard of the Factories Act or any of the other relevant labour legislation. Hired and fired at will, the workers worked long over the scheduled eight hour day at less than the minimum wage, and overtime was unheard of. There were no rest days, annual leave, medical, canteen or sanitary facilities as prescribed in the Factories Act. Aggarwal was on government contract and made vast profits by virtue of his cheap, limitless and unorganised labour force. All the workers, barring a handful, were immigrant *purabias*.

Fatehpur Beri was the seat of the local Congress Councillor, Mamchand. It is a large village and under his patronage a variety of small and medium industries had sprung up in its environs; it was also on the bus route to the lucrative sand quarries just beyond it to the south, on the border of the state of Haryana.

The farms around the neighbouring villages of Sahurpur and Chandan Hula were the seat of the local *toli* of the Dehat Mazdoor Union. The Sahurpur *toli*, as it was called, was the oldest, most steeled and most advanced in consciousness of all the *tolis* in the Union. The farm workers in this *toli* had long realised the need to organise and unite with the non-farm labour both in the villages and in the surrounding factories and quarries. They had friends everywhere, including Aggarwal's factory. When they heard about the conditions which prevailed there, they explained to the factory workers that they were much more effectively covered by legislation than the agricultural workers whose rights under the labour laws were still poorly defined, because they were still largely unorganised in the country as a whole. If the factory workers would only unite and organise themselves they could easily win at least their minimum legal rights and improve their present hand-to-mouth existence.

The factory workers were interested, but disunited and afraid of the *chamchas* and informers who would report any union activity to their employer and lose them their jobs at once. But, as we had experienced time and again, events did not wait for their preparedness. Six workers were arbitrarily fired from the

factory. Their mates, just beginning to stir under the influence of
their Sahurpur friends, decided to act. Five or six of them, led
by a tall, bony man called Ramdas who soon became their
leader, went to Mr Aggarwal and questioned the dismissal.

"*Sahib*," they said, "this can happen to us tomorrow. What
security do any of us have? We cannot be certain that we will be
able to feed our children tomorrow. Please take these men back
or they will starve."

The *sahib's* rejoinder was to tell them that they too could join
the other six. At this all the workers downed tools and walked
out in protest. Ramdas and three others ran to their friends in
Sahurpur, full of excitement and defiance and told them what
had happened. The Sahurpur Committee member advised them
to attend the meeting of the Executive Committee of the Union
that Monday evening, where a decision could be taken about
what steps to take next.

The Committee was not so pleased. Repeated experiences of
this kind had taught us that the first flush of enthusiasm could
rarely be sustained in the face of a long drawn-out battle. These
men did not really know as yet what unity was. They had acted
impulsively, without a thought to the next step. We asked them
what they wanted to do.

"That is for you to tell us. We are entirely in your hands,"
was the answer. That was too easy, we knew. But we had to do
something. Situations like this, with workers taking an impulsive
step and then landing the responsibility for resolution of the problem on the Union, were frequent and put us in a difficult position. We were not the usual kind of union with lawyers and
plenty of money to go to court with. Our Union was based on
the unity and consciousness of the workers alone. We had no
other support, and where this was weak or undeveloped, we could
make little headway. But the action taken by the factory
workers was also a positive step. Each such step meant a change
in consciousness, an advance from the prevailing silence of the
oppressed. But on the other hand it also exposed the selfish
opportunism of the uninitiated, their expectation that they could
transfer all responsibility to the Union. To them this Union was
a readymade institution, a business whose job it was to take on
just such cases as and when they occurred. They would pay us
for it, they assured us now, causing laughter all round.

So we explained to Ramdas and his mates what our Union was all about. We told them that the struggle for their rights must be based on their own unity and initiative. We would support them at every step but the burden of the struggle must be on their shoulders first. We would show them the way, but we had no readymade panaceas and they must be prepared for a long and hard struggle.

Then we pointed out the weakness in their case. They had taken a step which could be regarded as a strike. Under the law, they should have given 14 days notice of a strike after presenting a written charter of demands to their employers. A strike was the last step to be undertaken, not the first. In the lawless situation which prevailed in the factory, we felt pedantic telling them about these things, but we felt that they should know the facts. Bitter experience had taught us that the *maliks* in their lawlessness enjoyed an immunity the wretched *purabias* could never claim. It was ironic that while those who were illiterate should be penalised for their ignorance of the law, those who had all the privileges in a grossly unequal society could break the law and plead ignorance of it with impunity.

The factory workers had downed tools just before the month's end, and without their wages (which were certain to be withheld) they were hardly in a position to sustain a strike. So we decided that they should go back to work next day and present their demands to Aggarwal in writing. There were three immediate demands: that the dismissed men be reinstated, that the Factories Act be implemented, and that there be no victimisation. Unless these demands were met they would give notice of a strike in fourteen days time. We also reported the situation in the factory to the Labour Court.

But Aggarwal had anticipated his workers. When they went to work next morning they found the gates shut against them and a notice informing them that they could stay out unless they were prepared to sign a written apology for their misbehaviour. Locked out!

The Labour Inspector informed us that as Aggarwal had not even registered his factory he would be penalised for that, but until it was registered no action could be taken against him for violating the Factories Act. With the month drawing to an end, their pockets empty and no prospect of being paid unless they

submitted to the old conditions, it was either a question of total
surrender or a long drawn-out fight. The factory workers
decided on the latter. For the first three weeks all of them held
out in high spirits. Then, nagged by hunger, complaining wives
and children, with no signs of relenting from the *malik*, they
began to trickle back to work. Soon more than half—about forty
men—had broken the strike or lock-out (we never quite knew what
it was). Of these, some six or seven packed up and left for their
villages after signing their apology and taking the wages owed
them for the last month, and the rest ate humble pie and went
back to work. Their mates outside the gates were bitter and
angry at the betrayal. We tried to tell them that it was not
really a betrayal, only stark need, but they retorted, "Don't
we have the same need?"

The farm workers rallied round them. They shared their
scant meals, and when the factory workers decided to start a
dharna or sit-in at the *malik*'s house in Sarvodaya Enclave (it
happened to be next door to the ration office), they took food for
them all the way from their farms. But nothing moved Mr
Aggarwal, especially once work was resumed at marginally
improved rates for the blacklegs. The men outside, although
their numbers were dwindling as the weeks went by, refused to
give in either. We decided that they must divide into shifts.
Some would go into the nearby mines and quarries and earn
daily wages so that they could continue to eat, others would
stand guard at the factory gate while a third group would be
available for communication and contact. We tried to get them
to cook and eat together, as this would cut down expenses and
effort, but on this their age-old caste prejudices stood firm. For
the rest, a more gallant if exhausted little band of men and
women was hard to find. It had become a matter of prestige now
for all of them.

For two months they held out. There were rallies, demonstrations, and meetings every night at the factory gate. The villagers
of Fatehpur Beri took sides in the dispute which had attracted
wide interest all around. The village elite, some of whose relatives were in the factory management, sided with the owner, but
most of the others sympathised with the workers. Indeed, some
of them felt that we were too timid and should launch a physical attack on the factory owner. But we thought the most

important thing was to convince the workers who had returned to the factory to join the men outside again. We appealed to them every night, pointing out how they were injuring only their own cause by spoiling the opportunity they had to get the Factories Act implemented. We stressed that their salvation lay in their unity, that this was more precious than anything else, and that they must come out and admit their mistake in letting down their mates.

The workers inside used to line the factory wall and listen to us. They began to have second thoughts and approached us one by one—could they come out again? We told them that we would have the case settled very quickly if they did. But just as the tide was beginning to turn, two of Aggarwal's lackeys attacked and beat up Ramdas's wife and little son. The matter was immediately reported to the police who as usual did nothing. Ramdas and two others then demanded an explanation from the assailants. Their reply was to bring their *lathis* crashing down on the men. Ramdas ducked and avoided the blow, but little Sadhu went down with his head split open. This was the last straw. Egged on by furious villagers, the workers now turned on their attackers with a vengeance. The police arrived within minutes. They took the two lackeys and Sadhu off to hospital, and arrested Ramdas and three other workers for assault and rioting.

I got the news at about 10.30 p.m. from some of our Union men. We rushed to the DSP at the Hauz Khas police station near my home, knowing that the SHO Mehrauli would do nothing. The DSP suggested we ring the ADM, Navin Chawla. I did, and he promised that he would send his SDM the very next day to investigate our complaint. He suggested that we try and get our men off on police bail from the Mehrauli police station. Having no faith in the Mehrauli police we decided to get the men off on judicial bail in the court next day. But this matter of bail was another of our trials. Each time our people were arrested we had to get someone to stand bail. For that one had to produce sureties for Rs 2,000 to start with, and then this became Rs 5,000 and even Rs 14,000 as time went by and the authorities decided to make things more difficult for us. Where could a *purabia*, earning four rupees a day, stand surety for these sums? It was just one more blow at our attempts to get our rights. But somehow we managed to get enough people—from among the small pool of city friends and villagers with government jobs— to stand bail for the factory workers, and they came back full of fight from their brief sojourn in Tihar Jail.

"We must not be afraid of going to jail," they told their fellow workers. "You get a roof over your head and two meals a day—that's more than we get outside!"

But the others were apprehensive. The injustice of this latest episode had made some of them despair of ever winning through. We waited five days for the promised visit of the SDM. The men and their supporters sat on the sand heaps outside the factory in the scorching May heat. They had spent the past two months here, locked out of the factory where they were housed as well, unprotected from the sun which blazed down on them all day. Every day messages would be received from the Mehrauli police. The SDM was on his way. We must come to the police station at once. He had sent word that he was coming today. Every day hopes were raised, trips made to the police station and back, and all in vain. They were simply harassing us, it seemed.

Indignation was roused, and frustration too. We were in the middle of a meeting where it was being decided that we must force our way into the factory and occupy the place until our demands were met, when the SDM's jeep was seen coming up the road. He got out, mopping his brow and looked around for some shade. We told him that we had been on these sand heaps in the sun for the last two months and a few minutes now would not kill him. He reddened and blustered but then asked us to tell him what it was all about. On hearing the whole story, however, he had to admit that a grievous wrong had been done to the workers.

"Come with me now," he said. "Mr Aggarwal is sitting in the SHO's office right now. I promise you we will reach a fair agreement, and I will see to it that the men who attacked these people will also be prosecuted."

At first we refused. The workers were wary of these promises, and it was also a principle of our Union that we would not discuss any disputes in the police station, where the *maliks* invariably wanted us to meet. We said we had had enough diversions and deceptions and would now settle this ourselves. But the SDM pleaded with us to give him a chance to show us that it was possible to get justice after all. So Ramdas, his wife and son, the General Secretary of the Union and I got into the jeep with him and we drove off to Mehrauli, leaving the rest of the workers to wait for the result.

On the way the SDM tried to explain his delay. "I need my afternoon nap, you see. I'm so sorry to have caused you so much trouble, and made you wait so long."

Only five days, I reflected, and after two months of hunger, exhaustion and despair—and all because we want the Factories Act implemented. When we reached the police station there was no sign of Aggarwal. Duped again . . . . The SHO Mokhum Singh stretched his legs and yawned. He told the SDM there was nothing he could do about booking the men who had attacked the workers and Ramdas's wife and child because the x-ray reports showed only superficial wounds on all of them. If we wanted to take action we could go to the civil courts, he remarked casually. The SDM looked downcast and helpless.

He was plainly ineffective, we told him, as we got up to go. We were furious. The SDM looking more downcast than ever offered his jeep to take us back. We got in and the driver started up the engine.

"What happened?" he asked.

"Nothing. It was a wild goose chase," Ramdas told him. He shook his head.

At Andheria Mor, at the Fatehpur Beri turn-off from the main road some three miles away from the factory, we met the workers whom we had left at the factory gate to await the result of our visit to the police station. They had run all the way, hoping to catch us in time to be in on the settlement. Ramdas, our Secretary and I got out of the jeep which went on to drop off the woman and child at the factory. When we told the others what had happened they were stunned. Then they became furious.

"*Yeh gaddari hai*," this was treachery, they said. "He broke up our meeting and then deceived us. We want an answer from him."

"Let him call the *malik* now. We must settle this matter now," was the chorus. But the jeep would soon be back and it would reach the SDM before we could get to the police station on foot. He would simply drive away and we'd not see him again. So we decided to stop the jeep and ask the driver to drive back very slowly, through the narrow, crowded streets of Mehrauli, along with us.

When the jeep returned, we waved the driver to a stop and made our request to him. He told us that he could not do what we asked but offered to drive round another, longer way to give us time to reach the police station. This seemed too uncertain to us, so we asked him to phone the SDM from a shop and tell him to wait for us. He refused to do this, however, and just then the owner of a petrol station nearby, a Sikh who appeared to be a member of the Congress Party, came running up and offered to phone the SDM for us. We thanked him and settled down to wait.

What should turn up an hour or so later, but a police van full of *lathi*-wielding policemen who jumped out and set on the men without further ado. They scattered under the ferocity of the blows, but a small group held on, chanting steadily, *"Hum kya chahte hain? INSAAF!"* or "Justice is our Demand. Eleven workers and I were caught and pushed into the van, just as Mokhum Singh drove up in a private car. I will never forget the look of triumph and satisfaction on his face. After a fruitless attempt to catch more workers, they drove us off to the police station.

There, while I was searched by a policeman, each man was kicked and beaten viciously by the police when called in for registration. I caught a glimpse of the SDM who looked rather shamefaced but kept well out of the way. When I protested against this savage treatment and threatened to take the matter up in court, the police suddenly became polite and offered us cups of tea instead. But, bleeding and bruised and very angry, we were all under arrest. We did not know the charges, but hours later a police truck full of armed police arrived to take the men away, and Mokhum Singh armed with a pistol escorted me in a jeep to the Vinay Nagar police station which was the closest with a female lock-up.

It was my first experience of an arrest. The cell was dank and smelly. Two filthy, damp blankets were lying on a stone bench. The water basin and lavatory were dry and encrusted with dirt. I felt depressed. There was no sight of the sky, or trees or the sunlight. There was only this damp, gloomy cell with iron bars on the door and window, a huge padlock, and a sentry outside. To see people wandering about in the yard in front, walking in and out of office rooms, meant freedom. I was a prisoner and could move about only in this cell.

I sat down on the bench and thought things out. Then all the anger came rushing back at the sheer injustice of things, the blindness of those who could only react with brutality and force, the stupidity which made them immune to reason. Once again, with bitterness and anger, the realisation came to me that justice, a fair chance, a fair hearing, a fair *anything* was not for the poor and oppressed. And those like myself, once we declared ourselves unequivocally on the side of the poor, would be treated just like them. Well, it was just as well to know this and to have no illusions on that score. Rights? We had no rights. Laws? There were only paper laws for the people, meant to create an image of justice and equality. Try to implement them and you would soon discover the real intention of the lawmakers. So what alternative was there?

I spread the blankets on the floor, holding my breath against their smell, and lay down just inside the barred door where there was a faint breeze stirring. An officer had been deputed to sleep outside my cell, and after a mess of watery lentils and some thick *chapatis* had been handed to me through the bars, I tried to sleep. But the screams of a man being beaten in the cell next to mine kept me awake. At about 2 a.m., SHO Mokhum Singh turned up and unlocked my door.

"Come along," he said.

I didn't move. Anger surged up again. Now they had realised that they had made a mistake and wanted to let me go. I was damned if I'd go. We had decided earlier that no one would take bail and we would fight our case from jail.

"Come on, come on, your husband is waiting."

Charles, poor Charles, I thought, being hauled out at this hour! I went out and found Charles and Srilata standing by the desk of the duty officer.

"Listen Primila," Srilata said, "We've got bail for you."

"I'm not coming out alone."

"Listen, we have got bail for *all* of you."

"Everyone?"

"Yes, every one of you. We knew you wouldn't come out

alone, though they only wanted to give you bail at first. But we told them that was no good, so they eventually gave in." Srilata laughed. "They're in such a mess," she told me. "The administration realises that they over-reacted but the police are out to get you, and it's taken them hours to agree to let you out. The SDM is also here. He's sitting in his jeep feeling miserable, and says he doesn't dare face you!"

We laughed and went out. But I ignored the SDM as we got into the car and drove off. All the others were waiting for me at our home. We talked the rest of the night away and at dawn the men caught the first bus back to Mehrauli so that they could inform everyone that all was well and then return to town as we were to be produced in court that morning.

The SDM dismissed the cases for 'rioting and breaking the peace' against us as these were in his jurisdiction, and he promised us that the other charges would not be brought forward. We didn't know even then what charges there were against us, but we were happy to forget about them once we had been assured they would not be brought against us. The SDM, who was genuinely sympathetic. warned us that people were out to get us, and begged us to cool things and be careful.

Indeed, I was summoned by Navin Chawla not long after this.

"How dare you stop my SDM's jeep, Mrs Lewis!" He said angrily. "If this kind of thing doesn't stop I shall have you—and your husband too—externed from the Union Territory of Delhi, and no court will be able to revoke that."

I was shocked by the malice and hostility of the man. His threat to Charles, who was not involved at all in my work, was particularly objectionable and it exposed this petty tyrant for what he was—a man on the make who would stop at nothing to get where he wanted.

We realised now that in this unequal fight for the law we were too weak and isolated to hold our own. Although almost every political party had established contact with us and was eager for us to join it, our policy was that while all were welcome to work with us we would not join any party until we had tested it in practice. A brief joint front with the CPI(M) and the Socialist Party confirmed our doubts about politicians who only wanted to use us for their own ends. Lately, however, the CPI had contacted us and had been genuinely helpful in some ways such as giving us much needed legal help and knowhow. Now we felt that we must establish some closer links with them. We were by no means ready to join the party, but the workers agreed that in order to protect ourselves we needed to join a larger union and so we affiliated ourselves with the CPI-led All-India Trade Union Congress (AITUC) and the Khet Mazdoor Union as well. But more important by far was the recognition that we must expand our own strength in the area.

So the farm workers redoubled their efforts to spread out and organise other sections: the brick workers, quarry workers, stone workers—all existing under conditions of semi-slavery and bonded serfdom. In one place after another, among one section of workers after another, the flag went up and the see-saw struggle for the implementation of the legal rights of thousands of people began. In early 1975, we marched the twenty miles to and from the Prime Minister's house to bring to her notice the lawlessness of the employers in the Mehrauli *tehsil*. Along with two thousand brick workers, their wives and children and even their sheep and goats, we slept on the pavements outside her house and courted arrest the next day, forcing the non-plussed authorities to beg us to return in the buses they had provided for us, but not to turn the jail upside down with our numbers.

The day after this incident the police issued me with a summons from the court. The case of the SDM's jeep was being taken up after all. The charges were that we had threatened to burn the jeep and kill the driver. We tried to contact the SDM who had promised us the charges would be dropped. He had been transferred to another ministry and he evaded all our attempts to meet him.

Now we had to fight the combined might of the farm gentry, the village elite, the contractors, and the factory owners, who with the police and administration behind them, were determined to crush us. It infuriated them that because our activities were strictly legal they could find no legitimate way to stop us, apart from resorting to the shameful methods described earlier, of fabricating cases, making mala fide arrests and terrorising the people in any way they could. Now they decided to strike at the root of all their troubles—the leaders of the Union themselves.

On Monday evenings we held our weekly meeting of the Executive Committee of the Union sitting on tatty old hessian sacks on the floor in our office. This office was a tiny room at the back of a little store in the village of Satbari, and had been made over to us by the store owner, Kalu Ram. Kalu Ram was a refugee from West Pakistan who had settled in this village with his family some thirty years ago when the country was partitioned. They had seen better days in Pakistan, but had lost everything when they had to flee from there. Gentle folk, impoverished but full of dignity, they had observed the struggle of the *purabias* and had been won over to their cause. Although we still had the use of the *harijan panchayat* house in Sultanpur, it was not central enough and we had been looking desperately for a more convenient headquarters when Kalu Ram offered us the room behind his shop. He became an active Union member himself and was elected to the Executive Committee.

This shop was sandwiched between the houses of two contractors, both of whom wanted to get Kalu Ram out and take over the space occupied by his shop. One of them, Jit Singh, was a giant of a Sikh dealing in sand and the owner of two trucks. He saw us as a threat to his designs on the shop, and resorted to all manner of threats and harassment of our Committee members and to Kalu Ram in his attempts to get us out. He would frequently get drunk and disturb our meetings, try to start a fight and generally provoke us so that he could make it a law and order issue and demand our removal from the place. The village *Pradhan* was in league with Jit Singh, who was rich enough to bribe as well.

We refused to be provoked and made numerous complaints about Jit Singh to the police who took no notice as usual. One night he stole the Union flag which was tied to a pole on the roof of the shop. The workers were furious and took this as a deep insult, but we managed to calm them and reported the matter to the police. Although we had no faith in them whatsoever, we wanted it to be on record that we had kept scrupulously to the law and it was the other party each time who violated it. The workers made a new flag—a cement one this time, painted red, with the name of the Union carved out in white letters and a flame beneath it. The design was all their own and they had made certain that no one could steal their flag now!

One Monday night in April 1975 we were having an earnest discussion about democratic methods in our work. Each Committee member was going to have his say and as there were fifteen of us it was going to be a long night. Srilata and I had decided that we would stay over if we missed the last bus home, but this meeting was too important to be cut short.

At about 10 p.m., Kalu Ram and another man went out for a pee. They were rather long in returning, so someone went out to see what they were up to. He came back all excited and said that Jit Singh had accosted the two men, slapped Kalu Ram on the face and knocked the other man down when he had protested. The men rushed out, grabbing their *lathis*, and it was with great difficulty that we got them to come back into the office and not get into a fight. Jit Singh was drunk, he had a gang of *goondas* with him, and they obviously meant trouble. We sent off two men to the police station, demanding that they send a guard at once, while two others ran to ring up the Flying Squad and call them to the scene. The rest of us resumed our meeting in some tension.

A little later we heard sounds of whispers and laughter outside the door and opened it to catch sight of Jit Singh making off with one of the worker's *lathi*'s. This man and I now went out to retrieve it, and found Jit Singh and his gang standing outside the contractor's house on a pile of sand. When we asked him to return the *lathi* his answer was to bring it down with a powerful sweep of his arm on the *purabia's* head. Luckily the latter was able to duck and he disappeared quickly. I thought I might as well return to the office myself after that.

As I turned back, Jit Singh and his friends suddenly surrounded me and before I knew what was happening, Jit Singh had grabbed me by the hair, lifted me right off my feet, and thrown me to the ground. Then they began to work me over. I was too astonished to make a sound until a powerful kick in my ribs forced a loud cry out of me. This brought the workers and Srilata out of the office and they fell upon my attackers who quickly melted away into the night.

A bus passing on the road just in front stopped and the conductor leaned out to enquire if we wanted help. They took us to the police station where the police took down our statements and promised to send a squad out at once to apprehend our atta-

ckers. They returned after an hour with four of our Executive
Committee members whom they changed with trespassing into
Jit Singh's house. I was taken to hospital where the doctors,
after a word with the police, told me there was nothing wrong
with me. They gave me an injection and when I almost passed
out in a cold sweat they said it was just the shock. I was no
better after two weeks and x-rays showed that three floating ribs
had been fractured. I was advised five weeks of rest in bed.

Srilata met the new ADM for our area (Navin Chawla had
been promoted as special assistant to the Lt. Governor and was
soon to become the *de facto* head of the Delhi Administration).
This ADM told Srilata that the police had acted as they had
because Jit Singh's attack had been organised by some of the
most powerful farm owners in the area and there was nothing
anyone could do about it.

On 24 May 1975 I left for England with Charles and Karoki
on Charles's home leave. I would take my five weeks rest over
there. On 26 June the emergency was declared and Srilata and
twelve leading members of the Union were arrested. On 2 July,
on my return from England, I too was arrested at Delhi airport.
A week later in Ambala Jail, I read in the papers that the minimum wage for agricultural workers in the Union Territory of
Delhi had been raised to Rs 175 per month. Five rupees more
than what we had been fighting for.

3

"O but man, proud man,
Drest in a little brief authority,
Most ignorant of what he's most assured,
His glassy essence
Plays such fantastic tricks before high Heaven
As makes the angels weep."

Shakespeare

GETTING TO KNOW MY FELLOW DETENUE DR KAMLA Verma was one of the good things that happened in jail. We were together in Ambala for about three weeks, and then, one overcast monsoon afternoon, we were told that she was being transferred. After much hemming and hawing we were also told where she was going. She was being sent to the district jail in Karnal about fifty miles away. After about two months she returned to Ambala. We never knew why these sudden transfers were ordered. Perhaps they wanted to harass us, not let us settle down and 'adjust' anywhere, or perhaps they feared that we might get too close to one another and thereby present a more unified threat to the government. Sometimes of course, when the detenus became difficult for the jail authorities to handle, they were split up and transferred here and there on the demand of the jail authorities themselves. The orders came from the government and for no reason that anyone could think of, but the moment an order for a transfer was received the detenus concerned were packed off in such haste that often the jail to which they were going had no idea of their impending arrival and much confusion would follow in the attempt to get orders confirmed and the necessary facilities organised.

Kamla was forty-six years old, an *Ayurvedic* doctor by profession and a senior member and organiser of the Jan Sangh Party. The common image of the Jan Sangh was that it was a reactionary, communal and Hindu revanchist party with its ideo-

logical and organisational springboard in the Rashtriya Svayam
Sevak Sangh (RSS). The latter was regarded as an outright
fascist organisation with storm-troopers and all, and held responsible for the assassination of Mahatma Gandhi in 1947. The Jan
Sangh was the only party, apart from the communist parties,
which had a well-knit, highly disciplined, cadre-based organisation and a definite mass base which was concentrated in the
middle class, especially amongst the petty traders, shopkeepers,
and *bania* elements of northern India. The Jan Sangh also had a
concentration of teachers and students. The anti-Muslim and
anti-communist bias of the Jan Sangh and its support for Hindi
as the national language in a country of at least fourteen major
and distinct languages, combined to give it an unsavoury reputation for reaction and obscurantism. I too shared the general
opinion about the Jan Sangh and wondered how I would get
along with one of its leading members over a long incarceration
at what might become uncomfortably close quarters.

Kamla was fully committed to the philosophy of the RSS.
She insisted that the recruits from this organisation into the Jan
Sangh, which was a mass party, were head and shoulders above
the other members in their dedication, patriotism and discipline.
She explained Jan Sangh and RSS ideology and practice in a way
that was completely new to me. They stood for an independent,
strong and prosperous India rooted in its own rich cultural and
religious heritage. Hinduism meant far more than religion,
however. It encompassed the entire span of India's history and
included the land, rivers and vegetation, the sciences, arts and
philosophy, and all that was great and noble in thought and deed
since the hoary epoch of the *vedas*. Kamla said that our people,
80% of whom were Hindu, had lost sight of this past greatness,
had lost confidence in themselves as a race over the thousand-
year stretch of enslavement under Muslim and British rule.

"After all," she said, "let's face it, even the minorities, the
Muslims, Christians, Sikhs etc., are connected by origin, inte-
grally, to this common past, this Hinduism if you like. But the
Hindus themselves have lost all pride, all confidence in themselves, and the RSS is trying to build that pride and confidence,
that manliness again. The RSS instils discipline, dedication and
patriotism into its cadres, teaching them to revere every grain
of sand in this country as sacred."

I asked her why the RSS would not admit any non-Hindus into its ranks if it regarded them as an organic part of Hinduism. She said it was because the RSS believed it must put its own house in order first and clean out the Augean stables of Hinduism before it could lay claim to tackle anyone else.

I also put it to her that national pride and patriotism were all very well, but when 80% of our people did not have enough to eat we could hardly expect dedication and patriotism from them. What did they have to be patriotic about? The land, water and vegetation were all denied them; how could they, and why should they, hold every grain of sand sacred? The people who could make India free and strong were the workers in the factories and the peasants in the fields, and until we were able to change their lives we were worthless.

"Sacred grains of sand be damned," I said. "It's the *people* who matter."

Kamla agreed with me at once. By grains of sand she did not literally mean the soil but everything in this land, and that included the people of course. The Jan Sangh economic programme, with precisely these things in view, advocated a decentralised village economy and an end to monopoly and concentration of wealth in a few hands.

"We also believe in socialism," she said, "but it is our own, indigenous brand, derived from the *vedas*. You know, our great *rishis* and *munis* all spoke against greed and the amassing of wealth, of accumulating more than was sufficient for a man to live a simple and decent life."

We discussed the ruling party and its history during the independence struggle. Kamla said the RSS, founded in 1925, had fought for positive action against the British, and had opposed the compromising and conciliatory position of the Gandhi-Nehru leadership of the Congress Party which led to the Partition of India and the formation of Pakistan, a step which was the beginning of the end of the unity of India. Today, the Nagas, Mizos, the Kashmiris and Tamils were all trying to become autonomous or independent, and this was a betrayal of India's sovereignty. The responsibility for this betrayal lay with the leadership of the Congress Party which had weakly presided over the partition and dismemberment of the country.

"Atone time India's borders stretched as far as Cambodia in

the East and Afghanistan in the West, and look where we are today," she said.

"But Kamla," I protested, "that is exactly why people call you chauvinists. The whole of Asia is afraid of us, especially the smaller countries. They think we are expansionists and they are not far wrong. Look at our role in Bangladesh, Sikkim, and in Nepal and Bhutan as well. Every nationality has a right to its independence, no matter how small it may be, and by force and conquest, by coercion and oppression, you will only prepare a time bomb for yourself. Look what has happened in Bangladesh —the people there hate us. You can't go around 'liberating' people; they have to liberate themselves. And the way we moved in and started to throw our weight around in Bangladesh was just asking for trouble, and now we've got it. Even in our own country, until we can create the material conditions for the voluntary union of the Nagas and Mizos or whoever with India, until they stop feeling like second class citizens and 'backward' regions and 'scheduled' classes, we will never be able to unify them. And if we use force it will only rebound on us."

"But Primila," she said, "don't you see that as long as these minorities have extra-territorial loyalties, the Nagas to foreign Christian missionaries, the Muslims to Pakistan or Mecca or, for that matter, the communists to Russia or China, it's like having a fifth column in our midst. We uphold the right of every community to its own religious or ideological beliefs, culture and practice, but it should be contained within India's borders. I mean their first loyalty should be to India rather than to England, Pakistan or Russia."

Kamla went on: "They say we are caste-bound, communal, fascist. This is rubbish. We reject caste totally as a denomination by birth of one's place in society. We believe, for example, that a teacher is a Brahmin no matter if he was born a harijan. It is what you do that makes you what you are. We deplore the caste system as it has become, corrupted and degenerated from what it was in the beginning; it has only served to weaken and divide us. As for communalism, it is the Congress who has created the communal problem, though we are always blamed every time there is a riot. It is the Congress that has deliberately played a divide-and-rule game with the minorities, even with the harijans. It is nothing but a vote-catching gambit. They have, through

sheer opportunism, *created* the problem themselves in order
to have a secure vote bank with each minority, posing as their
only saviour and protector. And they distort our stand and
discredit us as communalists and reactionaries, when in fact we
believe that all should be equal, with equal rights and responsibilities. It is the Congress which has legalised discrimination
by having all these laws for separate representation and separate
rights for minorities."

Once again we were on delicate ground, because although
there was a lot of truth in what Kamla was saying about the way
the Congress had exploited the minorities and scheduled castes
question in order to secure their votes, it was also a fact that
there must be some protection of their rights in the face of a
dominant majority which would otherwise keep them at the bottom
of the heap as second class citizens, exploited and expendable.
No doubt during the thirty years of Congress rule the minorities
and the harijans had had nothing but a bad deal, but so had the
vast majority of the people, and even the pretence of secularism
was better than legalised religious or racial domination and
discrimination. Or was it? After much discussion we both agreed
that in fact no rights or freedom were ever 'given', they had to be
fought for and won.

Simple, warm and gay, with a lively sense of humour, Kamla
also had a seriousness, a curiosity and open-mindedness that
made her receptive, although always critically so, to new and
different ideas ranging from the political to the intensely personal.
We became very close as the months wore on. Married to a professor of Sanskrit, she had two sons and the family spoke only
Sanskrit in their home. Unlike most Indian husbands "Professor
ji", as he was called, had always encouraged Kamla to be independent, and throughout her detention he kept up her spirits and
inspired her to hold out and not lose heart, never complaining
about his own difficulties or pressing her to surrender. Professor
ji was also a staunch RSS supporter and was engaged at the time
in translating the Koran into Sanskrit.

Observing Kamla in our daily life together I found that she
invariably practised what she preached. There was no prejudice
in her, she was alert and sympathetic to the needs of all the prisoners, whether they were harijans, Muslims or 'caste' Hindus,
and she reacted to all forms of injustice with the same sense of

outrage as I felt. Our methods and approach were often different, reflecting the difference of our backgrounds, temperament and experience. Thus, where I tended to stress the collective approach to things she was less conscious of this and more individualistic in her methods, but through discussion and mutual consultation on all issues we were always able to thrash out differences and agree on a common course of action.

When Kamla was suddenly transferred, I was sad to see her go and she, not knowing what lay ahead and having become used to Ambala, felt even worse. But it was not until after she left that I realised that until then I had not really faced up to the implications of my detention. Putting a cheerful face on things, having been swept into this unexpected situation, I had simply been carried along, adapting rather than analysing, impelled by the daily course of events mechanically rather than by a realisation of the situation with a real command over it and myself.

It hit me for the first time with Kamla gone. I was distracted, confused and alarmed. I longed to be out, back amongst those I loved, wondering what they were going through, how Karoki was, where he was and how my parents were bearing up. Quite simply, I was rattled and could see nothing ahead. I had just been of the putting up a front and living from day to day.

Then, on 7 August, thirty-six days after my arrest, I had my first interview with my parents and my sister. They did not bring Karoki not knowing what to expect and thinking that the visit might upset him too much. They had received my postcard from the Delhi jail some two weeks before and had written numerous letters to me since then but none had reached me. Karoki was well settled in his new school and was quite happy there.

It was wonderful to see them, and they brought me a trunkful of books, all checked and signed for by a Delhi magistrate. Books were my greatest need at the time. We sat and talked and embraced, held hands and wept shamelessly in front of the deadpan ranks of CID men and jail officials who sat stolidly through it all. They had been granted permission to see me on special grounds of compassion or something, because interviews with detenues were not formally permitted until a month later. After that I saw them almost every week and Karoki came most times as well. Of course, only two visitors at a time were allowed, so they had to take turns to see me.

But after they left, a stream of warm, loving letters, full of courage and spirit followed, and these together with the reading matter I now had helped to restore my balance. I realised quite clearly that this detention might be a very long one, an indefinite one in fact, and that it was part of the life and struggle I had chosen for myself. There was nothing to regret, no cause for frustration. The fact that I was unable to continue that life and that struggle outside did not mean that it was not necessary to live and struggle here in jail.

After the first weeks and especially when Kamla returned from Karnal, we established a regular and disciplined routine. Exercise and baths followed morning tea, which came from the ward of our fellow male detenues who ran their own kitchen and fed us as well. Kamla would then sit for half an hour of prayer and meditation after which we had breakfast, normally consisting of a brass mugful of hot milk and two slices of bread each. Then we would settle down to work—reading, making notes and writing. Books from the jail library were mostly moral and religious tracts with a few colonial novels and some patriotic literature about the heroes and heroines of India. But once we managed to get books from our families our horizons expanded. These books ranged from biographies and writings of stalwarts of the independence struggle like Bal Gangadhar Tilak, Lala Lajpat Rai, Bhagat Singh and Vir Sadvarkar to the works of Vivekananda, Gandhi, Nehru, Marx, Engels, Lenin, Hitler, Golwarkar (the ideologue of the RSS), Prince Sihanouk, and Regis Debray. We read history, economics, literature and philosophy. The jail library provided one gem—a book called *Barrack Chaya* or *Shadow of the Barrack* by one Laxman Tripathi, a *Satyagrahi* and freedom fighter of the thirties. It was an account of his imprisonment during the struggle for independence in the dungeons of a princely state. His descriptions of the humiliations endured, the struggle of the political prisoners for their rights and of the gradual transformation of the criminal prisoners under the influence of the politicals was an object lesson and an inspiration to us both.

Kamla and I discussed all we read, and we agreed that we must read the exponents of various ideologies in the original in order to form correct judgements about them. All incoming literature was of course subject to censorship, but as long as we steered clear of oppositional writing and criticism of Mrs Gandhi, we managed fairly well.

In the afternoons it was oppressively hot during the summer and the electricity would be turned off. After lunch, which consisted of one vegetable and *dal* and *chapatis*, we would lie on our *charpais* swatting at the flies, reading or trying to get some sleep. Afternoon tea came at 4 p.m. and this, like most of our other meals, was shared with the matron on duty. After this we would exercise again, I doing the Canadian Air Force 5BX and Kamla a mixture of yoga with some of my exercises. Then, after a game of badminton or tenniquoits we bathed again, ate around 6 p.m. our dinner, consisting again of a vegetable or *dal* and *chapatis*, and afterwards took our evening walk round and round the yard, which covered about a square acre, for an hour or more.

The earth was bare, swept and swobbed twice a day by the female convicts. The high brick walls around the compound were bordered by flowering rose bushes and the barracks themselves were neat and freshly white-washed. There were two great trees, a *Bular* and a *Bor*, in the middle of the yard and from over the walls we could see the tops of *Peepul, Gulmohur, Neem, Amaltas* and Jacaranda trees—their splashes of flame red, yellow and purple blooms against the red brick walls, mossed over and dyed like some ancient carpet by the rains, made the surroundings very pleasant. The sky, clear or touched with clouds presented a pageant of golden, red and purple sunsets, and at night the moon and stars shone brilliantly through the leaves and branches of the trees. There was a variety of bird life, with squirrels and pigeons for constant company, and frogs and splendid spiders which came in the rains. It was more like an *ashram* than a jail; only the iron bars and padlocks, the clanking doors and the uniformed, baton-wielding warders were visible evidence otherwise.

During our walk around the yard after dinner we listened to the prisoners (who were locked up between 6 p.m. and 6 a.m.

every day) singing *bhajans*, after which they would often break
into more rousing folk songs and dances to keep themselves
entertained through the long evening before sleep came.

A major event of the day was the BBC Hindi service at 8
o'clock in the evening. Officially this was banned, but since we
were allowed transistor radios it was impossible to keep a check
on what stations we tuned into. Indeed the entire country was
tuned into the BBC during the emergency. Even Radio Pakistan,
also banned to us, was more interesting than our own "All
India Radio" as it had been dubbed even before the emergency.
The BBC was our only source of relatively objective news and
comment about the situation outside.

Of course there was also the underground communications
network between the detenus, not only in Ambala but with the
opposition outside and in other jails as well. But this was both
irregular and risky. We felt a strong sense of solidarity with all
our fellow 'sufferers', and though we were not allowed to meet
them we knew that we could count on their support and strength
through all the struggles that lay ahead.

Relations with our fellow inmates, the female convicts, were
somewhat ambiguous. According to the rules MISA detenues
were *nazarband*, or banned from view. We were to be kept
strictly apart from all other prisoners but allowed to mix freely
among ourselves. But no female ward in any Indian jail appeared to have separate facilities for political prisoners. It just
happened that in both Delhi and Ambala the office of the Lady
Assistant Jail Superintendent in the ward could be turned over
to us, but for any more than two politicals there was room only
in the cells or barracks of the common prisoners. We also shared
a common yard to walk about in, common toilet facilities, and
were in full view and earshot of one another. To try and keep
us apart in these circumstances was absurd and most of the
officers turned a blind eye on normal fraternising between us.

However, we found that both the matrons were constantly
giving the women surreptitious signals, glances and frowns with
the intention of driving them away from us whenever they found
us together. When we questioned them they would mutter something about "*Mana hai*", "it is forbidden", but would clam up

after that, especially when we told them that the officers in charge of us had said nothing of the kind. It was mystifying and created some tension in the ward, but at first we ignored the matrons, putting it down to mere officiousness on their part, and we went ahead in getting to know the common prisoners.

The *ashram*-like atmosphere of the female ward was enhanced by the quiet sobriety of the prisoners who were about twenty in number at the time. Now and again a burst of choice abuse in a quarrel behind the matron's back would reveal the lusty reality behind the nun-like exterior, but such quarrels were quickly suppressed and meekness would prevail again. The female ward in Tihar Jail at Delhi had been like a madhouse in comparison. We thought it must be because these women in Ambala were much fewer in number, and most of them were convicted prisoners rather than undertrials (those awaiting trials). This made good behaviour incumbent on them if they wanted to keep their records clean and earn their remissions regularly.

In fact, prison was a surprise. I had expected the worst in terms of overcrowding, dirt, brutality, rape, harassment and torture. But instead, here in Ambala at any rate, conditions were decent, well-ordered and clean. This was the immediate impression. The prisoners were attended to regularly by a doctor, made to keep the ward clean, fed substantially if monotonously, and not maltreated as far as we could see.

The passage of time brought other less salutary realisations. For example, the fact that most of these facilities were purely formal. The doctor came, but his stock of medicines was limited basically to aspirins, sedatives and digestive pills. These were applied indiscriminately and universally for all complaints. The better medicines, we were told, were given to the officers and sold on the black market or used for the doctor's private practice.

Similarly, whereas each prisoner was supposed to have half a pint of milk every day, the prison budget was being cut back and the milk supply was curtailed accordingly. This reduction of the budget would soon affect all supplies for the prisoners, and although their staple diet of *chapatis* and lentils was still relatively nourishing (Haryana being the 'granary of India'), it would not be long before the adulteration of even these basic foodstuffs became the norm.

Apart from this, we also perceived other aspects of prison life that over a period of time wore down a prisoner's dignity, self respect and faith in humanity. One of these was the attitude of the jail administration, officers and warders alike, that any work done for the prisoners was not part of the normal course of duty but a favour which could be withheld at will. Thus for the smallest things, such as buying a packet of *bidis* from the canteen with a prisoner's coupons (cash was not permitted to be kept and the prisoners were given coupons instead), or delivering a letter from her family, or recommending her for remission for work done, all of which form part of the job these officers and warders are paid to do, a prisoner could be kept in suspense for days, not daring to enquire too persistently lest the great one get annoyed. Such favours were 'goodwill' rather than the ordinary, routine dispensation of duty.

Of course 'goodwill' could always be bought. Corruption in jail runs a close parallel to corruption in the police. But this excludes all those who are too poor to afford bribes, and just as the rich can usually buy their way out of convictions in court, so in jail the relatively better-off prisoners can buy themselves an easier time than the majority of their impoverished fellows.

The second aspect we noticed was the absence of solidarity among the prisoners. Dependent on each other as they were, thrown together for years on end, inextricably bound to one another by all the circumstances of their daily life and work, they nevertheless stood alone, each one obsessed with herself, her own case, her own problems, and losing no chance to belittle, slander or carry tales about her fellow mates. Each seemed to despise the other from a position of virtuous self-righteousness. Although they felt each other's pain and depended on each other for company, there was no real friendship, no loyalty or trust between them. It was clear enough why. Solidarity among prisoners is the last thing a jailor wants.

Prisoners were encouraged to carry tales, to report on one another, to compete with one another for the warders' favour. There was a constant exhortation to remain *mast*, oblivious; the intention always being to separate, divide, isolate; to weaken and break the potential for solidarity, mutual support and trust. This of course is not unique to prison, but the effect on the human spirit, the cruel, dehumanising effect of these stratagems, came through forcibly in the prison situation.

My own instinctive need, from the first moments of my detention, was to reach across, to establish some human link. The
prospect of losing all identity as a human being, of becoming a
number, an abstraction, an object, was terrible. The need to
communicate, to put down roots and to draw some emotional
sustenance was overwhelming. It was difficult to appreciate that
these women, some of whom had been together here for seven
or eight years, had lived alienated from and hostile to one
another all this time. More so when their hunger for warmth,
affection, approval and friendship had manifested itself in their
relationship with us from the very beginning.

The long-term prisoners in the female ward were all under
sentence of rigorous imprisonment. All of them were of simple
peasant stock. *Tai* Rampiyari the *numbardarni*, or lifer in charge
of the ward in the absence of the matrons, had been in longest.
A wrinkled, upright old *Jat*, she was over seventy years of age,
with rosy cheeks, wicked little eyes and a toothless mouth which,
when she smiled, could still reveal the beauty that had once been
hers. She was as strong as a horse and did all the work the
matrons were supposed to do even when they were present in the
ward. *Tai* was charged with murdering her elder sister over a
land dispute. The prisoners all said that she was not really
guilty but that during her arrest she had slapped the investiga-
ting officer across the face because he had been abusive to her.
Vengeance being keen among the *Jats*, the officer swore that he
would see to it that she got charged with murder. She had been
inside for eight years now, never going home once on parole or
leave. Her record was unblotted and she could be let off any
time now according to the rules. When a lifer had completed
seven years in prison and earned three years of remission she
was entitled to a review of her sentence by the jail and police
authorities, and if recommended for release could be sent home.
The minimum time for men was ten years, but in either case the
matter rested entirely on the discretion of the authorities.

Also ready to go home soon were *Tai* Leela, her daughter
Bina, a suspected TB case, and her stepdaughter Shanti who was
in the third stage of TB and "sure to die" as the doctor cheer-

fully informed us. With them was Kamla's eight-year old son Subhash. They had been inside for over seven years. The three women had been convicted of murdering Shanti's husband. Subhash was three months old when he came into prison. He was a sharp-witted thin little boy, the same age as Karoki, reared amongst women convicts behind these four walls, with no schooling but so wise in the ways of the world. We christened him *Tau*, or uncle, and decided to teach him how to read and write. Despite his busybody ways he was a real child as well, chasing the squirrels and birds, teasing the frogs and spiders, crying when his grandmother bathed him and the soap got in his eyes. Everybody loved *Tau*.

Nirmala, sentenced for life for murdering her husband and two children, was also a *Jat*. She was a tall, proud, lovely young girl who had been beaten senseless by the police under interrogation. Barely over twenty, her whole life ruined, she was unpredictable in her moods—a disarming child one moment and a vicious, raging fury the next.

Maya, another lifer, was a strong, heavily built woman in her late twenties. She had been convicted along with her husband and brother-in-law because of a violent clash in a land dispute with her father-in-law and his brothers, in which one of the brothers had been killed. Maya had three small children at home and she thought of them night and day, just waiting for the time when she would be with them again. She was a sensible, balanced and dignified young woman whom I liked very much.

Phoolmati, the smooth-tongued *Banyani*, had been jailed for life for poisoning her husband because of a love affair with the local village doctor. She was about the same age as Maya, deeply religious, sharp witted and extremely clever with her fingers. Phoolmati and Maya were the only educated women in the ward, having attended the seventh or eighth class in the village school.

The swaying, slightly squint-eyed Dhanni had been sentenced to five years for kidnapping children. She was a bold, good-humoured, lusty woman of about forty, full of spirit and fun but with a vile tongue when crossed.

The undertrial prisoners were a source of curiosity and entertainment to the regulars of the ward. Every time the gate opened to admit one, women would crowd around demanding to know the details of her case, caste, village or town and personal life. The new entrant brought variety and a breath of the outside world.

For us, too, the undertrial prisoners were of interest. There was the young Rajbir, whom we christened "Pillo", meaning puppy. Arrested on a charge of *awara gardi* under the famous Section 169 of the Indian Penal Code for vagrancy, Pillo was addicted to *bidis*. She had to have one, she had sold herself for *bidis*, she told us artlessly. If refused she would roll on the ground, beat her head, tear her clothes and scream until the matron slapped and kicked her quiet. When you gave in to her just to keep her quiet, she would roll in the mud again, laughing and crying for joy. Pillo could not have been more than sixteen years old. She stayed with us a few weeks and then got out on bail provided for her by a constable in return for a spell with him as his keep.

This we learned was a routine occurrence. Single warders or policemen would offer to stand bail for these feckless young girls knowing that they were runaways, orphans and without help, in return for a temporary or long-term cohabitation. The matrons in jail, and the policewomen who accompanied the girls on their trips to court, acted as go-betweens and procuresses for their colleagues. The girls were only too willing to enter into these arrangements as they hated being locked up a day longer than they could help, and yet had nowhere to go once they were out on the streets again.

Little Paramjit the Majbi Sikh was brought in for jumping into a well with her daughter clutched in her arms. The daughter was drowned, Paramjit was hauled out and charged with attempted suicide and murder. She swore that she was in a *daura*, a kind of fit, when she fell into the well. She suffered these *dauras* every night. Her explanation was that her dead husband could not tolerate the fact that she was now living with his younger brother, and so every night he would 'take possession' of her. This possession, Paramjit told us, was literally a violent rape during which she gasped and moaned, her whole frame twitching and shuddering, this being the *daura* which all of us witnessed. She lost consciousness after this, and would be so exhausted the next day that she could hardly walk or even talk. The doctor injected Paramjit every evening with some strong sleep-inducing drug, but before long everyone realised that this was simply a ruse to get a medical report certifying her as mentally unsound or epileptic so as to be let off the murder charge. She was sentenced for life nonetheless, and was so shattered by the prospect of twenty years in jail that she hanged herself in the bathroom some months later.

Opium smuggling, pick-pocketing, traffic in women and children, vagrancy and murder were the most common charges against the women who came into the ward. Young girls charged with vagrancy told fearful tales of police atrocities while they were in their custody. The case of Meena was particularly tragic.

Meena came to us on a seven-day sentence of simple imprisonment. "She is mad," we were told. And certainly this attractive young Nepali gave the impression of being mentally unsound, throwing herself about, making coarse jokes, shouting curses, singing, grinning to herself, winking slyly at us or suddenly becoming quiet. But we realised that she could not be really mad as she was able to use the toilet, wash and clean herself, follow instructions and understand everything that was said to her. She was obviously deeply disturbed, however, and could not sleep at night, sitting up muttering, cursing, singing and shouting for hours on end.

Tai Bhagwanti, an elderly woman who had just come from the same jail in Hissar where Meena had been held under trial, told us her story. Meena had arrived in a fearful state, unable to walk, her rectum and vaginal area torn and bleeding, literally "hanging out," and raving like a lunatic. She had been kept in police custody for twenty-two days after her arrest, and every day she had been savagely raped by five or six policemen in succession. Practically deranged by this experience, she was then handed over to the jail authorities. She screamed and sobbed and threatened to jump on the *thanadar* or sub-inspector just as he and his cohorts had "jumped" on her. The sub-inspector of police shook his head sadly, "She's mad," he said, and the jail authorities had asked no more questions.

According to the regulations they should have refused to take custody of Meena until she had been medically examined on the basis of her complaint. They should have reported the matte to the proper authorities, after which a case should have been registered against the offenders. This is what should have happened but of course it did not.

When Meena was sentenced she was sent to Ambala. Here Swaran Kaur, the matron, locked her into solitary confinement where despite our protests she had to spend two terrible days and nights shivering in the damp, dark cell and screaming continuously. When the officer in charge of us came on a visit we demanded that she be let out or she might indeed go mad after her fearful experience. The officer ordered her out at once and she spent the next five days peacefully, with attention lavished on her by everyone. Her clothes were washed, her hair combed and oiled, and she was given the love and tenderness she needed so badly.

When her sentence was up Meena was sent off under police escort to the Nepal border. Two women constables and an Assistant Superintendent of Police were in the escort. She would be quite safe, we were assured. But who could be sure? And who cared? What was there to prevent the policewomen from being a party to further ravishing of the girl? She was poor, had no family and was at the mercy of all the forces of 'law and order', in the land. If she didn't fall victim at the hands of the police there were plenty of their kind in civil dress who would treat her the same way.

Meena had told us how, about six years before, she had been taken from her village in Nepal by a Brahmin (she was a Brahmin too), who had promised to marry her. He took her to Jwalamukhi in the state of Himachal Pradesh and installed her in his cottage. After a few weeks he began to drag his *manji* or cot outside the hut, and his 'friends' would be let in to visit the hapless Meena, who was warned to be good to them if she did not want to be thrown out. This is how she had been living when she was kidnapped by some *goondas* from whom she was rescued by the kind-hearted policemen of Hissar.

Meena is only one of thousands of young girls adrift in this country. Hungry for the good things of life, too poor ever to get them, they run away from home, or are put out or sold or given away to men who are supposed to marry them, but who put them to use as prostitutes, pick-pockets, opium carriers—anything to bring in a little cash. If they fall into the hands of the police they are used well before being thrown into jail. When they come out the same cycle is repeated again.

Was Meena's experience at the hands of the police exceptional? What about Gulshan, who came into jail unable to walk upright, saying shamefacedly that the police had pulled her legs so wide apart that she could hardly walk? And the timid woman who wondered if the jail 'police' would rape her like the police at the *thana* had done, tying her legs apart. And Bholi, caught 3 o'clock in the afternoon in Jagadhari and brought to the jail at 2 a.m. the next morning in a jeep with three policemen but no policewoman in attendance, and raped by all three on the way?

Any woman without sufficient escort or status was fair game, not only for assault by anti-socials of various kinds but by the police as well. Charges of vagrancy or loitering could be trumped up easily enough, and although these were taken none too seriously in the courts, the period pending trial and judgement provided ample opportunity for the police to have their fun at the expense of the hapless defendent.

The reasons for the ambiguity and confusion we had noticed in our relations with the criminal prisoners soon became clear. The officer actually in charge of the female ward was on a month's leave when we arrived in Ambala. Her name was Mrs Phool Kumari Singh and she was commonly known as *Behnji*. Mrs Singh was related to Bansilal, then Chief Minister of the state of Haryana (where we were jailed) and who later became Defence Minister. Bansilal was notoriously corrupt, arrogant and vindictive. A firm supporter of Mrs Gandhi and her son Sanjay, he had placed himself and the whole state of Haryana, which he ruled like a despot, at the service of the personal needs of the Prime Minister and her son, thereby putting himself beyond reproach or enquiry, and thus regarded as one of the most powerful men in the country. A member of Indira Gandhi's infamous caucus throughout the emergency, Bansilal was also one of its chief architects.

Mrs Singh came in for her share of power by virtue of her relationship with the Chief Minister. Her word was law whether she was absent or present as we soon learned. Unfortunately, though not unexpectedly, Mrs Singh took it upon herself to carry the political war between the ruling party and the opposition into the female ward as well, and tried to harass us by putting what obstacles she could in our way, and denying us communication with the female convicts. Since the rules said that there was to be no intercourse between MISA detenus and ordinary prisoners, Mrs Singh could legitimately take this stand. But equally we were able to point out the absurdity of trying to keep us apart unseen and unseeing, when we shared a common yard and other facilities and were in full view of each other night and day. What was accepted as common sense by all the other officers, however, was intolerable to Mrs Singh. The lengths she went to in order to have her way and exert her authority over one and all were absurd at first, but developed into a long nightmare of tension, fear, cruelty, struggle and revolt.

Both the matrons competed for Mrs Singh's favours and worked as domestic servants for her, spending most of their duty hours attending to her at her house. The major part of their free time was also spent working for her so that, exhausted by their labours even before they came into the ward, all they did was to lie on a blanket under the trees and have themselves massaged, oiled and deloused by the criminal prisoners.

Sita, the elder matron, was boss—at least to begin with. Not only was she senior, with twenty years service to Swaran Kaur's four, but she was also Mrs Singh's favourite. Swaran Kaur, on the other hand, was insecure about her job, not having been confirmed in it as yet, and desperate to please. Hated by Sita, who it seemed had poisoned Mrs Singh against her, she was bullied and exploited mercilessly by both.

For the first six months of our stay in Ambala Mrs Singh was on leave for a month at a time throughout, coming to work for sometimes as little as three or four days before she went off again. The much vaunted 'discipline' under the emergency certainly did not affect her. In her absence two senior officers, who were in charge of the detenus, took charge of the ward as a whole. They were pleasant, courteous and efficient, one or both coming round almost every day to see if all was well and if we needed anything. We asked if we could teach the women to read and write, do physical exercises, play games etc., and they said by all means, they would be grateful if we could do something for

the prisoners. They even promised us a Hindi primer so that we
could begin our teaching.

But we found that every time we started something with the
prisoners, and were found together with them when the matrons
came into the ward after doing their stint for Mrs Singh,
the glances, signals and gestures would begin. The women,
smiles and laughter frozen, would slink away from us, silent and
unhappy. While the matrons were out of the ward, everyone
would relax and we were able to chat and joke with one another,
get on with our lessons, and help each other in little ways. A *bidi*
or cigarette for one desperate for a smoke, scissors for another
to cut out a shirt, needles and thread to sew a tear, milk, bread
or fruit for someone with a small child or another who was sick
and so on. They in turn, and especially Maya and Phoolmati,
the two lifers who were the most skilful and reliable of the lot,
would insist on washing our clothes and bed sheets (which were
made of heavy handspun cotton), filling our water drums from
the tap and cleaning our room. Although I wanted to do my own
work, Kamla, who was not very well, was relieved to let these
strong young women give her a hand.

Sometimes we would join in the songs and dances of the
prisoners and listen to their stories of life in the village or the
experiences of opium carrying, pick-pocketing and other petty
crimes, forced upon them by poverty and unemployment rather
than choice, it seemed, in almost every case.

At last Mrs Singh's return to duty was announced. The
female ward braced itself. She entered one evening while I was
taking my walk around the yard (Kamla had left for Karnal).
She looked very young, slim and quite attractive, but at closer
quarters I saw that she must be in her early thirties, and
her face was pinched and sour. She was self-conscious and greeted me with an over bright, "You have come from Abroad; take
me to England with you." I continued my walk, ignoring her
after a brief, "I'm glad to meet you at last. I have heard so much
about you." She, over eager, "What? What have you heard?" And
I, "Oh, only nice things." A chair was rushed forward for her
and she sat down for a few minutes surveying with a frown
the quickly assembled women gathered around her.

"Have you been behaving yourselves?" I heard her ask. "You
had better now that I am back, hadn't you?" She swept out after

that, and the women looked apprehensive. "Now it will begin again," one of them muttered as I passed.

After that we did not see her for several weeks and she was on leave again after a few days in the office. But now piles of her dirty clothes began to come in to be washed by Maya and Phoolmati. It seemed this had only stopped when we first arrived, perhaps because Mrs Singh was ashamed to have it done in our presence. But she apparently found it impossible to get her clothes washed by jail *dhobis*, who could not do the job half as well as these young women, and who would have to be paid besides.

Apart from washing, Maya, Phoolmati and Nirmala now also resumed another job they did for Mrs Singh. Every day they sat for hours bent over a bed cover, sheet, table cloth, sari or some other garment, doing the most painstaking, fine embroidery while the matron on duty hovered over them to see, as I was told virtuously, that the girls did not complain or grumble but performed these tasks as a "labour of love". The girls, cursing and groaning when the matron had gone told me, "If that *rand* ever gave us a word of appreciation, just one kind word in return for all this work, we'd do it happily. But what do we get? *Didi*, if you knew what this woman has done to us, what she is like— may God be our witness."

They called me *Didi*, meaning older sister. But they did not dare to tell me more about Mrs Singh at first. They would only shake their fists and curse, "May she die a dog's death. Our curses will reach heaven. God will hear us some day and He will surely deal with her."

And they went on washing and embroidering day after day. Their work was so professional that Mrs Singh would have had to pay a fortune in the market for it. But as I soon found out, she had even stopped work coming to them from the jail factory, for which they would have been paid, so that they could get on with her private work, which was strictly illegal in any case.

The background for this state of affairs was revealed to me after the dramatic incident with Nirmala. During my first interview with my parents, Mrs Singh had been among the jail officers presiding over the meeting. I had asked the Jail Superintendent if my mother could send me an adult literacy manual with which I could teach the women inside. He raised no objections and nor did anyone else.

A few days later the book came by post, and I gave it to Nirmala and Subhash who were the most eager to learn. Full of excitement, they settled down to work at once. All day and late into the night I heard their solemn, earnest voices slowly making out the words and sentences.

Two days later I was reading in my room when *Tai* Rampiyari the *Numberdarni* came in quietly, put the book down on my table and turned to go without a word.

"What happened, *Tai?*" I asked.

"Nothing," she whispered.

"But Nirmala needs that book," I said.

"No, no. You keep it, she has returned it to you. She has finished with it." *Tai* was very nervous and hurried out of my room.

A little later the ward door opened with a clank, and looking out of my window I saw Saroj holding Nirmala up and leading her towards the prisoners' barrack. I went out onto the verandah and saw all the women huddled together outside the barrack. They were very quiet and no one looked in my direction.

After a while Sita came into my room. She was solemn.

"You shouldn't give these people anything," she said.

"You mean that book?" I asked. "You know the officers gave me permission to give them that book. And besides, what harm can it possibly do?"

She shook her head, "That milk you gave Joginder's son, I warned you not to. It only gets the women into trouble."

She avoided mentioning Nirmala, and the reference to the milk was merely an evasion of the subject. A word about that, however. At first I used to give the milk that came for me every morning to Subhash. Then a woman called Jogindro and her two year old son came in and the boy fell sick. He was unable to digest the thick *chapatis* and oily *dal* which was the prisoners' staple diet, and so I gave him the milk and bread instead. The matrons tried to stop me. It was forbidden, they insisted, refusing as always to tell me who forbade it. I told them to go to hell. I would take the responsibility for giving this child milk and bread. They could go and tell that to their *Behnji*. She was carrying things just a bit too far with her remote control over the ward and its affairs. Why didn't she come and see to things herself? Do her job for a change? If they could ever be around when the doctor came, for that matter—if the matrons saw to their duties for a change too—they might be able to see that the child was put on the hospital diet. I was angry and threw caution to the winds. I knew that all this would be reported to Mrs Singh and that she would make things even more unpleasant for us all, but I was tired of being polite about the absurd restrictions she was trying to enforce in the ward.

Now something serious had obviously happened to Nirmala, and it was connected with the literacy manual I had given her. I was sure of this. Mrs Singh always exerted her authority, threats and vengeance on the prisoners; not once did she ever approach me directly. The matrons and women in the ward had been warned that I should not be told what was going on. But the tension and anxiety this caused me and the isolation I felt, especially while Kamla was away, when the women were forbidden to speak to or even smile at me, was, I was sure, quite calculated.

After the women were locked up in the evening and the matron had gone off duty I went across to the prisoners' barrack. This was the only chance in the day to talk properly to them, although the fear of stool pigeons amongst them was a restriction on free conversation. The ward remained unattended for three hours every evening, from six to nine o'clock when the night matron would come on duty. Actually this long period with no matron in the ward was against regulations, and risky too in case of a crisis in the barrack like a fight breaking out or someone falling suddenly ill. If we detenues had not been there to run to the door and call for help, as we had to many times, no one would have heard the shouts from the barrack until too late. But nobody could tell the matrons off, or insist that one of them remain in the ward till the other came on duty, because everyone knew that they had to go to Mrs Singh's house to cook her dinner. However, for us it was a time of relative peace. It afforded a chance to talk to the women, standing outside the window of their barrack, sometimes for two and three hours at a stretch, and often having to dodge the matron who took to coming in earlier than usual at night, and very quietly, in order to try and catch us out.

The women were waiting for me on this occasion, bursting to tell. They said that Mrs Singh had sent for Nirmala in her office. She was to be taken out very quietly so that I would not notice anything. In the office Mrs Singh had fallen on her, abusing her violently for taking the literacy manual from me. She had broken two canes on Nirmala's arms and then, losing all control, she had hit her about the head till the girl fell down practically unconscious and had had to be helped back to the ward by the trembling Sita. Both of them had been warned that there would be more trouble if I came to hear so much as a whisper of what had passed.

Nirmala, pale and very quiet, was lying prostrate on the floor; the women were terrified and outraged.

"*Didi*, this woman is not human, she is a *rakshasa*. She never stops to ask, just brings down her cane on us. . . ."

"But this is monstrous," I cried. "She has no right to do this to you. She should have spoken to me if she had any objections to my giving you the book—she was present when the officers said I could get it for you—she could have objected then. This is outrageous. And what earthly harm is there in your wanting to learn to read and write? I'll speak to the Superintendent about this."

Then the whole story came tumbling out.

All of them tried to speak at once, but Phoolmati got a vantage point behind the barred window and was able to make herself heard above the din.

"*Didi*, don't say anything to anybody, it's no use. She is Bansilal's sister-in-law and everyone, including the IG *sahib* himself, is scared of her. She can do what she wants and no one has the guts to question, let alone stop her. You are new here, *Didi*, you don't understand this place. If you knew what we have endured these past three years. . . . All our letters have been stopped, she tears up all the letters we write to our families and theirs to us. Punni brought us a pile of torn up letters to show us, when she was pretending sympathy for us. We get no remissions, no coupons for work done—we have got nothing, absolutely nothing for these three years. We use to card three kilos of cotton, our full quota for the day, and we also had to embroider her saris and shawls and things, knit sweaters for her and her daughter, her friends and relatives, wash piles of their dirty clothes. Our eyes have become weak doing that close embroidery, and she gave us so much to do that she even stopped the cotton coming to us from the factory so that we could spend all our time doing her work. And what have we got for it? Just kicks, insults, beatings, abuse—nothing else. The other prisoners in this jail are treated so well. They get proper remission for the work they do, they get paid for it every month, they get letters to write home and their people come to visit them and bring them what they need. But we in this ward are denied everything. Oh *Didi*," Phoolmati's voice cracked, "you don't know, nobody knows how we have passed these last three years. Our *karmas* are *khota*, we are ill-fated. But God will punish her. He will not let our curses go unanswered. She will die a dog's death."

"But why?" I asked, "there must be some reason. Something must have happened to make her like this. She can't just be completely mad."

"It's those other *rands*—that Punni *chudi* and that Swaran Kaur. They have poisoned her against us. They carry all kinds of false reports and gossip about us—she demands it from them in fact, and she never comes here to investigate anything herself, you can see that yourself. Has she ever come into this ward since that first time? Did she ask you about that book? No, she only loves to listen to *chugglies*, lies and false reports so that she can beat us up. We can stand anything but these beatings. We can't do anything when she doesn't stop to listen but just brings that cane down on our heads."

Phoolmati began to cry, and some of the others too wiped their eyes.

"My dear friends," I told them, "you alone can stop that. If the officers are too afraid, and the matrons are in league with her then you will have to defend yourselves without their help. She is acting totally illegally if what you say is true. She has no right to do this to you, and that she is able to get away with it in his name is no credit to Bansilal. But you have to take some action. If you keep quiet no one will ever know and she will just go on torturing you. The woman seems to be insane and you will have to put a stop to her madness yourselves."

"But how?" they wanted to know. "What can we do? Who will listen to us?"

"When the Superintendent comes on the Tuesday parade to inspect the ward you speak up," I told them. "Tell him what's going on and demand that the jail rules be applied to you as they are to everyone else. If you haven't done wrong you needn't be afraid of speaking up and demanding your rights."

"But *Didi*, haven't you seen what happens at the parade? She has warned us that we must not ever complain or say a word against her to anyone. We have orders to keep our mouths shut, eyes down and remain absolutely still at the parade. Why, she has even forbidden us to let you get any wind of this. That day Swaran came and shouted at us—"Why did you let her *feel* something has happened?"—Remember that first time when we all stopped talking to you? The matron had ordered us to stay away and not say a word to you. Do you think we would ever behave that way of our own accord? We feel so bad, you are all alone now, even *Mataji* has gone, but we have been forbidden to go near your room, to talk to you and even to greet you." They called Kamla *Mataji* or Mother.

"But don't you see," I told them, "the very fact that she is so anxious to hide these things means that she knows that she is in the wrong. So why not expose her and demand redress?"

Phoolmati beat a fist against her forhead and Maya pushed her stout frame forward, saying, "Do you think the officers will listen to us? Is it not the Superintendent's duty, when he comes here every Tuesday for the parade and sees our blank tickets, to ask why our remissions have not been entered? Is it not his responsibility to find out, to ask *us* why we are not getting our remissions or coupons? What is the parade for if not to find out what problems we have and if all is well in the ward? All these officers know very well what is going on; they just don't have the nerve to question her or us. So we have no hope of redress."

"But my dear girls," I said, "don't you see? Why should an officer or the matron or anyone outside bother to ask questions and raise a hue and cry for you when you yourselves are silent? If they are scared of her they will be even less likely to do so. *They* aren't suffering, so why should they stick their necks out

for you? Unless you gather the courage and determination to
raise the issue yourselves you won't get anywhere. Even if they
know something of what is going on here they can pretend that
they know nothing as long as it is not brought to their notice.
And you alone can do that. *You* are being wronged, not they. If
the child doesn't cry how will the mother give it milk?"

"But how, *Didi*? If we so much as open our mouths that
Phool Kumari will beat us to pulp and that we cannot stand."

"You can resist anything, all the illegality of this woman,"
I told them, "but only if you act together, raise your voice as
one and protest against what is being done to you. Discuss it
among yourselves and come to a decision, all of you together.
You know the rules better than I do; you know what has been
done to you and how the rules have been violated. You can
explain all this at the parade and demand redress. But only if
you stand together as one and back each other up."

How often had this been proved in Mehrauli! Slowly the idea
sank in, but the worst obstacle to their unity was their lack of
trust in one another, the mutual suspicion, lack of affection,
a selfish preoccupation with their individual interests. They
were unable as yet to see how defenceless they were, how hopeless it was to protect even their own individual interests unless
they learned to cooperate with and support one another, unless
they developed faith and trust in one another and made a
common stand.

"If we could unite," Maya said, "if we could speak with one
voice, of course we would solve the problem. But that is just what
we cannot do. We are too foolish, too selfish and afraid. If one
of us speaks out no one will back her up. If one steps forward
the rest will step ten paces back. Let the one who sticks her
neck out risk the noose, why should the rest of us? That's the way
we think. So let us mind our own business, let each one see to
herself. If anyone feels the need let her speak up for herself, but
to ask us to depend on one another and to back each other up is
impossible."

After a few days we noticed that Nirmala was beginning to
droop. Gradually her face lost all colour and became quite white.
She stopped eating and refused even to take her tea. She said her
head hurt, maybe as a result of the blows she had received from
Mrs Singh. She told us that Swaran Kaur threatened her every

day, saying that as soon as *Behnji* returned she would be strung
up from a tree and beaten till she dropped. She could not stand
it any more. If this did not stop she would die, she said.

I decided to speak to the officer in charge. It was a risk
because the matron on duty was supposed to be in attendance
when any male was in the ward, and although they had seldom
bothered to observe this rule in the past, they made sure to be
present now when the officers came on their rounds, suspecting
that I might say something about the state of affairs in the ward.
The problem was how to tell the officer what was going on without saying anything to compromise either the women or myself.
The situation had reached a stage where the slightest evidence
to prove that I was 'fraternizing' with the criminal prisoners
would be used against us by Mrs Singh and establish her right to
punish the women. The letter of the law was on her side in
this case even though common sense and humanity dictated
otherwise.

When the officer came on his evening round I told him what
had been done to Nirmala because of the book I had given her,
and demanded to know why this could happen when he himself
and the Jail Superintendent as well had allowed me to give it to
her in Mrs Singh's presence. She could have made her objections then if she had wanted to, but what she had done to a helpless prisoner was intolerable.

He was shocked by what I told him, "It can't be as bad as all
that!" he exclaimed. Then he went over to the prisoners' barrack
and spoke to the women. Nirmala fell weeping at his feet and
begged him to transfer her out of this jail as Mrs Singh would
not leave her alive here. She told him what had happened and
also that Swaran Kaur's daily threats were terrifying her. She
was so weak now that she could not stand up by herself and had
to be helped to her feet. The officer sent for the doctor and his
examination proved that Nirmala was in a state of shock and on
the verge of a nervous breakdown. She was sent to the civil
hospital in the city and stayed there for three weeks under
sedation.

While the doctor was examining Nirmala, the rest of the
women gathered the courage to speak to the officer about their
other problems as well. Phoolmati and Maya told him how their
tickets had been taken away from them without any explanation

by Mrs Singh some four months back. These tickets are the
record of each convict, and for a 'lifer' they are life itself. A
spoiled ticket, a bad report or charge against the lifer can mean
years added to her sentence. The women complained about the
way their letters had been stopped, remissions and coupons
denied them, and begged the officer to look into the matter and
help them.

He asked the matron where the tickets of Maya and Phoolmati were. On being told that they were "lost", he had new ones
made out for them and promised that the rest of their complaints
would also be looked into and put right.

"As long as the female ward is in my charge," he told us as he
left, "you can rest assured that there won't be room for any
more complaints. But after that I cannot promise anything."

That was to be the refrain of all the officers from now on.
The implications were clear. While Mrs Singh was on leave
there was peace and some kind of justice, but no one could
vouchsafe it once she was back at work. Relief and gratitude
were therefore mingled with apprehension. The women said that
Mrs Singh would be furious when she found out what had
happened, and prove quite capable of wreaking vengeance on all
concerned, including the good officer.

Swaran Kaur soon resumed her threats again, taunting the
women about their new found daring, and promising them that
things would be put right as soon as Mrs Singh returned to
work. But the women, having gathered the courage to speak up
once, now let nothing pass. They even made a formal complaint
to the Superintendent at the Tuesday parade. They told him
about Nirmala and the matron Swaran Kaur's threats and
abuses, and after getting confirmation from me as well he
promised to sort things out and told them not to worry.

But when Mrs Singh returned from leave, she ordered the
tickets of Phoolmati and Maya to be brought to her office, tore
them up, produced the original tickets which she had seized four
months ago, and concocting totally false charges against the two
girls recommended that they should be produced before the
Superintendent for punishment. This was the dreaded *paishi*.
Even Sita, the senior matron was shocked. "It's too much," she
said shaking her head, "She has gone too far."

"But Sita *ji*," I urged her, "you can speak up about this and tell the truth. Tell the Superintendent that these charges are false. The whole ward is a witness that no such incidents took place. We will all bear witness to the truth."

She laughed mirthlessly. "Haven't you learned anything yet? Just watch and see what happens."

Even though she was Mrs Singh's favourite, the women preferred Sita to Swaran Kaur because she was able to handle them herself and did not carry tales and reports about them to Mrs Singh. Swaran Kaur was not only unable to manage the prisoners, but being desperate to keep her job, saw her way to it only by insinuating herself into Mrs Singh's good books. By carrying tales and reports about everything that went on in the ward to her, Swaran Kaur was able eventually to oust Sita and become Mrs Singh's stooge. The charges against Phoolmati and Maya had been made on the basis of her reports, and this single, totally mala fide action could ruin the hitherto spotless records of the two girls.

The entire ward was shocked and angry. The women said that this meant that Swaran Kaur and Mrs Singh could concoct any charges they liked against any one of them, and it would be entered on their tickets. None of them would be spared if they let this happen.

I was glad that they were at last beginning to see that the situation affected them all. But I counselled patience now, and that we should wait and see if the Superintendent took any notice of the charges. He had assured us that we were not to worry about Mrs Singh.

Her next attack was on the officer who had tried to put matters right in the ward. She complained about him to the Superintendent and to the IG (Prisons) as well, accusing him of having a vested interest in coming to the female ward, taking bribes from the detenus and flirting with the women. She demanded that he be banned from the female ward altogether. The women were even more outraged by this, and they refused to do her work that day.

Infuriated, she ordered Maya and Phoolmati, whom she saw as the prime offenders, into her office, and charged them with rebellion against her. She said she knew that they were being incited by me and also by the officer in charge of the detenus who had looked after the ward in her absence. She tried to force the two women to confirm her charges against him. When they refused to do this and insisted that the *"Dipty Sahib"* had only tried to implement the rules, she lost all control.

"Rules!" she screamed at them, "You'll soon know what 'rules' you'll get—and that bastard, he'll know all about 'rules' soon enough too. I'm not afraid of rules. I'm not afraid of any-one—be he the Superintendent, the I.G. or God himself. I'll see how any of you leaves this place alive, just you wait! You think those *daphter wallis* can help you? I'll see how they get out of here too!"

She raved on, hysterical with fury, but she did not raise a hand on them. This was a triumph for us. She had not dared to strike them, perhaps because of the fuss and commotion over Nirmala's beating which had resounded throughout the jail and even out-side, when the girl had been hospitalised and others came to know what had happened. Mrs Singh's threats about the *'daphter wallis'* was a reference to us detenues who were using her office or *daphter* to live in.

But apart from her threats the fact that she had not dared to raise a hand against Maya and Phoolmati was grasped slowly by the prisoners, and I tried to convince them that they must drive this advantage home. They must refuse to do any more of her private work, and demand that the Superintendent make a proper investigation of the charges she had made on the tickets of the two women. It was slow going; they saw that they must make a stand against the injustice being committed on them but they were so afraid. And with good reason. There is no more helpless being than the long-term prisoner.

Kamla came back from Karnal about this time, and it was a relief to have her with us. We felt better able to resist Mrs Singh, and for the two of us it was especially good to be together again. The long, lonely days in Karnal had taught her patience and she was more composed and strong than she had been before.

We talked to the matron Sita about the situation in the ward. She was a shrewd and experienced woman, hardened and unsentimental after twenty years in the prison service. We were curious to know what she felt about the struggle between the prisoners and Mrs Singh. She told us that we were a pair of innocents taking everything on trust the way we did. We were ignorant about the deviousness and cunning of the women prisoners, who deserved all they got. Sita said that Mrs Singh had been quite different to begin with, and very naive. But the deceit and deviousness of the prisoners had made her hard and vindictive. If the women had not been so eager to curry favour with her and carry tales about one another to her, the situation need never have become as bad as it was now. Blind to common sense, the women had even tried to play one matron off against the other and report on both to Mrs Singh, thus losing the trust and goodwill of one and all.

"Don't trust anyone here," Sita told us. "Just wait and watch and learn. Phool Kumari is foolish and has no idea how an officer should behave. She does not know how to handle these women and has lost all balance and control over herself. She is childish and vindictive and thinks that because she is related to Bansilal she is God herself. But are the others any better? You should see the way the officers, from the most junior right up to the top—with maybe one or two exceptions—fawn on her and try to win favour with her, just because of her connections. They are all vermin. All of us are, and you are simpletons if you think you can do anything to change the situation."

Sita's advice was that we should mind our own business and keep out of trouble. But she was too cynical to convince us. Even if she was right about the weakness and venality of the women, we felt that they had become like this because it was the only way they knew to survive. If they were rotten, poverty, want and desperation had made them so. But here in jail they were helpless, and Mrs Singh was taking monstrous advantage of their helplessness. Instead of trying to understand and help them to overcome their weaknesses, she had become a sadist and seemed out to destroy them. Something must be done to stop her.

We had a long talk with the women and they told us their version of the background to the present state of affairs. It seemed that about three years before we came, Phoolmati had fallen seriously ill and had to be sent to the civil hospital in Hissar. With her went Shanti, the lifer who had contacted TB and who also had to be hospitalised. While there, Phoolmati struck up a friendship with a man called Pyare who was a relative of Shanti's, a lifer himself and also in hospital at the

time. Pyare and Phoolmati decided that they would get married
as soon as they got out of prison.

This simple and perfectly natural development is not taken so
easily in a feudal and authoritarian society like that of India. It
created a scandal. Phoolmati was a *Banyani* from the trader caste;
Pyare was a *Gujar* and tilled the land. Moreover, Phoolmati
was serving a life sentence for the murder of her husband. She
was a widow with the stigma of murder on her brow. Although
she was not even twenty years old at the time, for her, life was
over. To think of love and marriage, and in prison at that, was
outrageous.

When Phoolmati and Shanti returned to Ambala, the latter
lost no time in telling the whole ward, the matrons, warders and
Mrs Singh as well, about what had passed in Hissar between
Pyare and Phoolmati. Mrs Singh, who was the victim of a failing
marriage herself, seized upon this evidence of 'sin' and became
quite hysterical. She abused and belaboured the girl, jeering at
her immorality. Phoolmati, terrified at the possible consequences
of her romance, denied having had any such relationship and
insisted that Mohan was only a childhood friend who had been
good to her when she was ill. This apparently enraged Mrs
Singh further. She caned and beat Phoolmati every day for two
weeks and forbade her to talk to or mix with her fellow prisoners.
Her letters were stopped, her money taken away and when her
relatives came to visit her they were so insulted by Mrs Singh
that they left vowing that they would not come back.

Completely isolated and desperate, the girl had been on the
verge of a breakdown with no let-up in the daily administration
of abuse, beatings and threats from Mrs Singh and the matrons.
In this situation Punni, the cleaning woman or *bhangi*, had
stepped in, and with a show of sympathy had persuaded Phoolmati
to write a letter to Pyare who was still in Hissar, telling him
of her plight and asking him to help in getting her transferred
back to Hissar. Punni told her that she would give Phoolmati the
postcard to write on and post it for her too.

Phoolmati wrote not one but five desperate postcards to
Pyare, telling him what Mrs Singh was doing to her and begging his help. Punni delivered these postcards to Mrs Singh. It
seems the whole thing had been a trap for Phoolmati. Now all
the long-term prisoners came in for Mrs Singh's wrath. She

insisted that all of them had conspired with Phoolmati to "spoil her good name" in this way. Maya especially was a target for her fury, because it was with her pen that the postcards had been written. She was beaten as well, and all of them were now prevented from writing or receiving letters and from getting their coupons and remissions for work done. The reign of terror had begun.

"Sita is right," Phoolmati said, "when she told you that we are our own worst enemies. If Shanti hadn't talked none of this would have happened. And afterwards too, when all of us were being treated in this way by Phool Kumari, do you think it ever occurred to any of us to protest or resist her? No, we competed with each other to flatter her and get into her good books instead. Each thought, if only I can please her she will favour me. And the only way to keep her happy is to fill her ears with gossip and reports about one another."

The women told us that before we came and took over her office, Mrs Singh used to come in to the ward at about 11 o'clock in the morning, lie down on a *charpai* in her office and get the women to massage her two at a time while they gave her all the gossip. They had to make endless cups of tea for her and the matrons out of their own stores of tea, milk and sugar, and they had to go on pressing her legs for four and five hours at a stretch with her never once asking if they needed a rest. Then, after beating up whichever one of them she felt like, she would go home at about three or four in the afternoon and they would not see her again until the next morning at the same time. She never did a stroke of work, it seems, and no officer dared to come in while she was there or to check what she was doing.

At home, too, the matrons told us, she would not lift a finger to help herself. She couldn't even make a cup of tea, and if her friends dropped in after the matron had finished up and gone home to her own family at last, Mrs Singh had no compunction about sending for her again just to make tea for her visitors. It was incredible that this state of affairs had gone on for so long unchecked and unquestioned merely because of Mrs Singh's connections.

The situation was particularly ironic in the face of daily newspaper and hourly radio proclamations that under the emergency all indiscipline, nepotism and corruption had been wiped out. We stressed this in our exhortations to the jail authorities to put a stop to the illegal activities of Mrs Singh. They would only shrug their shoulders.

"Nothing's changed, in this state at any rate," they told us. "You should know the politics of Haryana. Don't think we don't know what is going on and don't sympathise with these poor prisoners, but we are helpless. We can't do anything, because we would only risk being suspended or even losing our jobs if we did. She would charge us with favouring the detenues or some such thing, and that would be it."

It was not surprising, therefore, that the women were convinced that nothing could be done about the situation. Yet we knew, and they did too, that much did lie in their own hands. They could go on hunger strike and refuse to work until their just demands were met. They might have to endure punishment, but it they held out they knew that they would win in the end. Even the jail rules had it that an officer must be removed if the prisoners brought sufficient evidence against him.

But the women had to move at their own pace. At the Tuesday parade Maya and Phoolmati, backed stoutly by Dhanni, brought forward their complaints again to the Superintendent. He assured them that he was seized of the matter and they had nothing to worry about.

That evening the doors swung open and Mrs Singh walked in twitching her cane. She had a chair brought for her near the main barrack, sat down and called the women to her one by one. We watched anxiously from our verandah. At first it appeared that she was only checking their jail uniforms, the first bit of work we had seen her do since our arrival. Then she called Dhanni, who had been the most outspoken about her that morning at the parade—a fact that had no doubt been reported to her by now. Dhanni came forward and stood in front of her and the cane swung into action. It was very quick and the blows did not look very hard, but Dhanni, who suffered from a prolapse and needed a major operation, collapsed after this beating. Mrs Singh sauntered out after announcing loudly enough for all of us to hear that the rule of her cane was the only 'rule' this ward would ever see, and any officer who dared to intervene in the name of "rules" would get a taste of the same.

She turned up again next morning and on hearing that

Dhanni was prostrate, she kicked her, swore more abuses and threats and warned her of worse to come if she complained or called the doctor for treatment.

The woman seemed to be drunk with the arrogance of her power, but frightened too, especially of us detenues. She knew that we were aware of everything that happened in the ward, that we had an influence on the women and, as far as rules and regulations went, on the officers as well in that they knew that they could not allow things to go too far without risking an outcry from us. She knew, too, that we would not let a word of this go untold once we got out, and although she hated us for being a threat to her even when we were prisoners ourselves, she did not have the nerve to vent her malice on us directly. But her attacks on the women seemed to be a show of force to prove to us that no one could stop her. She wanted to provoke us into some direct intervention so that she could prove that we were 'inciting' the women against her, but we gave her no chance to do this. And although she was afraid that she might overstep the mark she was goaded on by her overweening arrogance, stupidity and hunger for power, and infuriated by the growing defiance of the women which she saw as entirely our work.

After Dhanni's caning we told the women that they must resist Mrs Singh's attacks by stopping her hand and holding her until an officer came and took charge of her. We explained that this would not constitute an attack on an officer, which as we knew was a serious offence. It was sheer self-defence against a criminal who had been let loose on them, and if no one else could stop her they alone must and could do so.

But it was too big a step to take. The women told us that their only weapon was collapse. They could fall sick, give up eating, weep and wail and create a drama like Nirmala had done, but they could not stop her hand directly.

When the Deputy Jail Superintendent came to see us that evening, we told him what had happened and that we felt that Mrs Singh was criminally insane and had no right to be let loose on helpless prisoners. Why not put her in charge of us? we asked him; *we* would be able to deal with her. He laughed and said that she would never agree because she was frightened of us; because of us, she had told him, she did not want to come into the ward.

While we were talking Dhanni staggered up, assisted by two

women, and fell at his feet begging the "*Dipty Sahib*" to protect
her from Mrs Singh. She was telling him what had passed when
the ward door rattled and the doctor was announced. This was
lucky coincidence. The DSP had the doctor check her, and she
made an instant impression when she lifted her skirts to show the
purple and black marks on her thighs where Mrs Singh had hit
her. There was much shaking of heads, and the DSP muttered to
the doctor as they went out after noting Dhanni's case that "the
woman" should be committed to a mental asylum.

After this it was arranged that Mrs Singh must be accompanied by the Head Warder or an officer when she came into the
ward. This was explained as being necessary for her own protection, but it was clear that the tension in the ward and the potential danger of the situation was at last having some effect on the
authorities. A month later she was promoted to the rank of
Deputy Superintendent in charge of the Factory. The grounds on
which she merited this promotion were only too clear, but it was
a tactful way of getting her out of our ward, and for this we
were grateful. A few days after this, Bansilal was made a minister
in the Central Government, and the whole of Haryana heaved a
sigh of relief at the removal of the tyrant. In jail we danced and
sang in celebration, thinking that now at last there would be an
end to Mrs Singh and her doings.

But the lady caused the damage she had sworn to do. In a
flurry of changes, just at the time when the tension in the ward was
at its height, the I.G. (Prisons) and the Jail Superintendent were
both suspended. Rumours flew that Mrs Singh was responsible,
and she herself gave full credit to the gossip. The jail administration was in a paroxysm of fear, and she utilised the opportunity
to force the Acting Superintendent, no other than the DSP who
had had Dhanni examined by the doctor, to sign the charges she
had made against Maya and Phoolmati. Too frightened to refuse,
he did as she demanded and the fate of the girls was sealed.

Nothing could be done to remove the blot set on their records
by this act of spite which could result in extending their jail
terms by up to two years. This was the last straw for Maya and
Phoolmati, who now refused to do any more work for Mrs Singh.
Even when she was no longer in charge of the ward, her washing
and materials for embroidery continued to stream in, but now the
girls would not touch it. The matrons threatened and cajoled in

turn, but to no effect. Frantic with worry they had to set about the job themselves, with *Tai* Rampiyari the faithful *Numberdarni* the only one prepared to help.

The officer who was given charge of the ward in place of Mrs Singh was a good man who forbade any private work being demanded of the women. He also restored their rights to correspondence and remissions, and for a brief spell we tasted the relief of normality.

It soon became clear, however, that the new dispensation was not strong enough to withstand Mrs Singh's determination to plague the prisoners. As DSP (Factory) she now began to load them with so much work, cotton to card, mattresses and quilts to fill up and sew for the winter which was now upon us, straw to be plaited and weaved on to the seats and backs of chairs: there was no end to the stream of work she piled on them. They filled and exceeded the set quotas, after which they were due both rest and payment, but she saw to it that they got neither. Even though their 'task sheets' were duly filled in and signed by the officer in charge of the ward, Mrs Singh refused to countersign them, insisting either that the women had not done as much as was necessary for payment or that they had done a bad job. She was determined to prevent their being paid for the massive quantities of work they so patiently and carefully completed every day in the hope that now at last they would get a fair deal for their labours. When the women began to murmur and protest to the matrons and warders, she would hold back work for one or two days every so often, and then say that she could not recommend any payment because she had not sent in any work at all.

Although it was clear that she was lying, nobody was able to challenge her. The new Superintendent, weaker and more cowardly than his predecessor, simply did not want to hear about it. He would rush in and out of the ward every Tuesday for the parade, not giving anyone a chance to open their mouths to make a complaint.

These Tuesday parades in the female ward were a farce anyway. According to regulations, the Superintendent was supposed to inspect each ward once a week to check if all was in order, if the wards and inmates were clean, and to hear any complaints or questions that might be raised. But in the female ward this

parade had been reduced to a mere formality. While Mrs Singh
was in charge she had not bothered to attend it although she was
accountable; the Superintendent on his part had never once
inquired why the tickets of the prisoners, held up in front of
their faces for him to examine, were blank, with neither remissions nor comments to explain their absence on a single one.
Once the women broke their silence, however, he was forced to
give them a hearing and reassure them. He was also embarrassed by us politicals who were supporting the prisoners, and he
knew that in a crisis all the inmates of the prison, including the
other detenus in the male ward, could make trouble for the jail
authorities. We had already informed our fellow politicals of the
situation in our ward, and had arranged a signal with them in
case of real trouble. But although the jail authorities were
aware of the potential for a revolt and were anxious to avoid
one, they were too paralysed by fear of Mrs Singh to be able to
take the simple steps necessary to restore peace by giving the
prisoners their normal rights.

Thus their only recourse was to try and evade the issue and
run away from the problem. It was laughable to see the new
Superintendent streak into the ward every Tuesday, rush past the
assembled women, then come nervously into our room where he
would ask if we were well, and before we had time to answer,
shoot out with a flurry of officers and warders stamping to attention and shouting "Clear the way for *Sahib Bahadur*", finally to
disappear through the doors of the ward which had been flung
wide open to let the dignitaries out.

However, with Mrs Singh no longer in charge, there was
some relief for a time, and we were able to turn our minds to
other matters until the next crisis blew up.

Soon after my arrival in Ambala I had made a writ petition to
the Delhi High Court, challenging the validity of my detention
and demanding to know on what grounds I was being held
prisoner. Thousands of detenus all over the country had flooded the High Courts with similar petitions, and the judges were
not only admitting them but had even ordered the immediate
release of some people. Kuldip Nayar, editor of the big English
daily *The Statesman*, had just been released, and the government,

embarrassed and infuriated at the prospect of large numbers of people being set free in this way, quickly moved the Supreme Court to remove the right of Habeas Corpus altogether. A new Chief Justice who was committed to Mrs Gandhi had already been appointed, and now the government set about shuffling the judges in both the High Courts and the Supreme Court by transferring or superseding most of those known for their independence and integrity, and replacing them with others who would be sure to toe the government line.

But before the Supreme Court made its expected judgement in support of the government's plea for the suppression of Habeas Corpus, there was a ding-dong battle between the judiciary, struggling to protect its rights and sovereignty in constitutional matters, and the government which was now ruling by ordinance and decree, but which still wanted a rubber-stamp parliament and judiciary to legitimise its actions.

I was summoned to Delhi by the High Court while this battle was at its height and before the ruling of the Supreme Court put an end to it. With tremendous excitement at the thought of seeing the outside world again, being able to meet Charles and some of my friends at the court, and above all of seeing Srilata again in Tihar, where I would be put up for the night, I set out by police van under an armed guard at about 5 p.m. on 19 January 1976. I had no hope at all of being released because I knew that the government had closed all the loopholes in MISA and their detention orders on which grounds alone I could have been released. My lawyers could only plead that my detention order had been served without due "presence of mind", i.e., literally because of some error in typing my name, address or place of arrest on the detention order itself. But I knew that the police would merely hand me a corrected version and I would be back under arrest in minutes.

With my writ petition I had prepared a statement (See Appendix) about the nature of my work and commitment which I had hoped would be read in court. But it soon became obvious that this was impossible when the 'grounds for detention' were not permitted to be discussed in court, and Habeas Corpus itself was suspended. However, copies of the statement were cyclostyled and circulated privately during the emergency.

However, I did expect to see my relatives and friends and to be able to talk to them freely without CID and jail officers in attendance. I had seen Charles fairly regularly since his return to India in October 1976, although it was hard for him to take the day off to come and see me on Thursdays, which was the day for interviews in Haryana prisons, and which meant a long ride by coach or car from Delhi each time. But friends were not allowed to visit at all, and this would be the first time, perhaps the last, too, for a long time to come, that I could meet some of them. There was a tight knot of excitement and anticipation in my stomach right through the long journey to Delhi. As it was already dusk when we started, my hopes of seeing something of the outside world through the barred windows of the van were disappointed.

The driver kept to a speed of twenty miles an hour, and when I asked why we could not go faster he laughed and told me that I was "precious cargo" and he did not dare risk any mishap to me. The police escorting me were kind and jolly. More relaxed than in the early days of the emergency, they talked freely of their discontent and the oppressive burden put on them by the emergency. With prices going up again, their own wages unchanged, duty hours doubled and nothing else changed, they found themselves at the rough end of the stick and were fed-up with hounding people at the behest of the rulers, and earning only fear, hatred and contempt in return.

We reached Tihar Jail, Delhi, at one o'clock in the morning. Srilata was waiting for me. She had been told by one of the officers that I was due that day and had been waiting since the morning. Now I would only have a few hours with her as I was to leave for the court at nine. She had cooked a delicious meal for me, but we could hardly eat for the excitement of being together again. We exchanged our experiences and found that both of us were prepared for the prospect of an indefinite incarceration. Neither of us was ready to surrender to the government and try for a conditional release, despite the fact that we had been told by our families that the two of us were special targets for the malice of no less than Mrs Gandhi herself because of our work in Mehrauli.

We talked until I left at nine o'clock when I was informed that my escort had arrived. This time it was the Delhi police who were in command, and they came in an open truck. I clambered into the front seat with the driver and a policeman, and we drove in the hazy winter sunlight through the well-remembered streets of the city to the High Court.

As the van pulled up at the court gates a man came running up and whispered to the Assistant Sub-Inspector in charge of the guard over me. I was asked to remain in the van while the ASI went to check something. I saw some of my friends, who looked strained as they waved to me but would not come nearer. We waited a while, then the ASI came back and told me that there was a little problem with the magistrate who was insisting, on behalf of the Delhi Administration, that I remain 'in camera' and not meet anyone as I was a "danger to the state", while the Registrar of the High Court, on behalf of the Judiciary, claimed that I must be free to move and meet whoever I wished as long as I was in the precincts of the court.

We waited some more time and then I was called into the building. In the office of the Registrar I found Charles, my lawyer and the friends who had come to meet me. The magistrate from the Delhi Administration was also there, looking rather embarrassed. He was arguing with the Registrar that I must not be allowed to meet these people as I was a "highly dangerous person". The Registrar tried to reason with the man and at last, taking a deep breath said, "I'm sorry, but I must ask you to leave my room at once." He was addressing the magistrate, who left in some confusion. The Registrar also asked the police to leave the room. Then he turned to me.

"Mrs Lewis, you are at liberty to talk freely and in private, to move wherever you wish within the grounds of this court and there is no one who can deny this right to you. That man," he indicated the magistrate, "is a personal friend of mine but I had to throw him out."

My friends cheered him, and we were able to talk to one another without interruption after that. First my lawyer, Mr Har Dev Singh, went through my file and showed me the defence the government had made in reply to our submission that I had been detained without reason, grounds, or legitimacy. The key line in the defence was that I was "a well-known political activist who had held demonstrations" etc., and this, as Mr Har Dev Singh told me, was all they had against me. Since before the emergency was declared it had not been illegal to be

a "political activist" or "hold demonstrations", the charges
were hardly substantial. It was clearly a case of malice, the
lawyer told me. Har Dev Singh was a top-ranking advocate who,
like a few other brave colleagues, had taken on the defence of
various MISA detenus like myself, free of charge. They were
brave because they risked harassment, threats and even detention from a government which was determined to stamp out
every source of dissent and resistance to it.

Charles showed me a letter from my mother in which she
wrote that she had gone to see Mohammed Yunus, a friend from
pre-partition days in Lahore, who was now one of Mrs Gandhi's
closest confidantes and a special envoy. He had told her that
there was no chance whatsoever of Srilata and I being released.
We were dangerous communists, he said, and moreover I was a
CIA agent married to an Englishman for "political" reasons. He
called half a dozen cabinet ministers communists too, and said that
there was a deep-laid communist conspiracy in the country which
had to be crushed. My mother commented on the demented state
of the man, his paranoia and sheer stupidity. Yunus told my
mother that "they" were particularly angry with me and would
keep me inside even after everyone else was set free.

With this in view, Charles and my friends tried to convince
me that both Srilata and I should write to the government and
ask to be released on reasonable terms. They reminded me that
we had no party to back us up, we had been working as
individuals and were defenceless against the malice and might
of the ruling family.

They had a point, and I had to recognise the truth of what
they were saying. Both Srilata and I were in jail only because we
had aroused the ire of some of the most powerful people in the
country. We had been warned time and again that we would be
in serious trouble if we crossed Mrs Gandhi, whose spite and
vindictiveness were a byword. But both of us were loathe to give
in. We did not want to accept conditions for our release when we
had done nothing wrong. I suggested that we wait and see how
things developed. At least let us wait till the others were released.
There were thousands of people in jail and some time, somehow,
the situation was bound to change.

My appearance before the judge was brief. The court room
was very full, and I was in such a daze that I hardly knew it had

begun when the proceedings were over and I was led out after being given a date for the next hearing. But now I was back in the jurisdiction of the police, and they hurried me out and into the waiting truck with time only to say a quick goodbye to my friends and Charles.

I was taken back to Tihar where Srilata and I had some tea and a last exchange. Then I had to go. The Haryana police were waiting to take me back to Ambala.

On 28 April 1976, by a majority of four to one, the Supreme Court ruled in favour of the government's petition to forbid all writs of Habeas Corpus. The dissenting judge, Mr Justice Khanna, on cross-examining the Attorney-General Mr Niren De, was informed by him that "if a District Magistrate has a personal grudge against an individual, the former can deprive the latter of his life without redress or remedy". Mr Justice Khanna, who was the senior Supreme Court judge, resigned in January 1976 after being superseded as Chief Justice by Mr Justice Beg, one of those who had supported the govern· ment's petition.

Ambala was a relief after the tension and strain of the excursion to Delhi. We arrived after midnight and Kamla was waiting up for me with hot coffee and a snack. I told her all that had passed and also that I had met her party colleague, Pushpa Kale, and a number of other Jan Sangh women in Tihar. There had been no time to talk to them at any length, but they all sent their greetings to their comrades in Ambala.

Pushpa Kale was to join us quite soon. She turned up one cold February morning at 3 a.m., having been transferred from Tihar along with some five hundred other detenus because of a successful jail-break made by twelve lifers. The Tihar Jail had a capacity for two thousand prisoners. Under the emergency, five thousand had been packed in without any corresponding increase in jail staff. The resultant chaos, lax discipline and security, and increased corruption made it easy for the twelve men to escape. They had bored a tunnel 75 feet long, we were told, from the factory to the outer wall and beyond.

We were delighted to have Pushpa Kale with us. A tiny little woman, full of fire and energy, she gave us welcome support in the struggle against Mrs Singh which had again reached a critical stage.

As DSP, Mrs Singh was now able to take charge of the jail whenever the Superintendent was away and his place filled by the senior DSP who was in charge of the administration of the whole jail and of our ward as well. With the senior DSP as acting Superintendent, Mrs Singh could take his place and assume charge of the female ward as well. She lost no opportunity in doing this in order to harass and browbeat the women convicts and perpetuate her sway over the female ward. Moreover, during this period the administration of the jail was subjected to a rapid turnover of senior DSP's, and each new man, knowing that he would remain in the post for a few weeks or months at most, was anxious not to take any step which might bring him into disfavour with the authorities. Each one remained content to let things slide, refusing to take any decisions of a controversial nature and passing the buck to the next man along the line who did the same in turn.

Mrs Singh, who had been festering under the restraints imposed on her dealings with the prisoners, now persuaded one of the new deputies to give her charge of the female ward once again. This time she took charge of us three detenues as well. Once again we braced ourselves for combat.

The first thing she did on taking charge was to send for Nirmala. The matron Sita, who had fallen out of favour with Mrs Singh during the last crisis for having refused to carry tales and report on us, took the girl in to Mrs Singh's office. Nirmala was trembling with fear when she went but came back full of excitement. She told us that Mrs Singh had bade Sita remain outside, asked her to sit down in a chair, laughed a lot and told her that she was to be appointed Mate, her task being to supervise the others in their work from the factory, watch that the matrons did not steal any goods and report regularly to her on all that went on in the ward. In return for this, she would not have to do any work herself and would be given coupons, kept supplied with *bidis*, matches and anything else she needed.

Then Mrs Singh had called Sita in and informed her that Nirmala was now Mate and would report directly to her (Mrs Singh). She forbade all tea-making in the ward, a small luxury which, though strictly illegal, was allowed by most officers who simply turned a blind eye on it. She also demanded to know where we had got our *angithi* or little coal stove from. Sita told her that the officers had permitted us one on which to heat up our food.

"I'll see about that," Mrs Singh promised.

She also sent for Maya's ticket, and struck off the entry assigning her to work for us made by the officer last in charge. She said there was no need for anyone to work for us.

Kamla had chronic piles and was suffering from severe pains in her neck and shoulders, later diagnosed as cervical spondilitus. Pushpa had back trouble and had been struck down by a severe attack of spinal pain after her arrival in Ambala. It was impossible for either of them to wash the thick hand-spun bedclothes, sweep and clean the floors and carry the heavy iron buckets and drums to and from the water tap. They had been allotted this help on medical grounds, and there was no question of it being taken away. So too with the little stove on which we heated water for the hot water bottles Kamla needed when she was in severe pain, and on which we made our tea and warmed the food which became quite cold, now that it was winter, by the time it reached us from the male wards. As far as we were concerned, Mrs Singh could make little headway and she soon relinquished charge over us. She didn't last a week, in fact. But the convicts were another matter.

When Nirmala returned, full of triumph and excitement from her visit to Mrs Singh, and told us what had passed, the women were full of dismay. Nirmala as Mate? they said; why, she was a mere child. The most junior of them all, she had no right to be Mate. The older women, especially *Tai* Rampiyari and *Tai* Leela were indignant.

"We have got grey hairs in jail and now this chit is going to lord it over us? It is intolerable!" they said.

Even worse than the unfairness of the appointment was the fear that Nirmala, who was unstable, childish and very stubborn, would let this elevation go to her head and bully and ride roughshod over the rest. If anyone dared to complain about her she would carry false reports to Mrs Singh and get them into trouble.

Kamla and I could not believe that Nirmala, who had suffer-

ed so much at this woman's hands and of whom we were so
fond, would betray us, and we tried to make her see what harm
would follow if she became Mate. The women tried to persuade
her to refuse Mrs Singh's offer and to tell her that she could not
do the job with such senior prisoners as *Tai* Rampiyari and *Tai*
Leela around. They said that with only eight or ten long-term
prisoners liable to do factory work anyway, it was unnecessary
to have a Mate at all.

But Nirmala's head had been turned. Dreaming of the power
she would now have over everybody, she began to show an
aspect of herself about which all the women, and the matrons
too, had long since warned us.

"I am a Jat," she spat at us, "and Phool Kumari is a Jat.
Say what you will, I'll stand with her. I *will* become Mate.
Don't try to remind me of all that I have suffered at her hands
—I'll say I suffered nothing. She did nothing to me, that was all
an act—it was these women who made me do it. They led me
on. That's what I will say. And watch out, if any of you gets
funny with me you'll be in trouble. Phool Kumari will listen to
anything I say. And I'll say nothing against her even if I have to
rot here for twenty years. We are both Jats, and blood is thicker
than water."

Nirmala had turned traitor. It was hard to believe, and the
spite and vindictiveness which she now displayed were a revelation. Sita laughed at our disbelief and dismay. "What did I tell
you?" she said. They're all the same. Each one of them will bite
the hand that feeds them without hesitation if they think it is
to their advantage. I've lived with them for twenty years and I
know what I am talking about."

Nirmala instituted a whole range of new regulations on
orders from Mrs Singh. No prisoner was to leave her *charkha*
for any reason whatever until the full eight hours work was
done. If anyone wanted to go to the toilet, or feed her baby or
just stretch her legs for a moment, Nirmala would come out of
the cell in which she sprawled on a *charpai* all day now, and
shout threats and abuses at the woman concerned, saying that
she would be reported for malingering and punished by Mrs
Singh if she so much as moved from behind her spindle.

The Master from the factory, another of Mrs Singh's
stooges, came every day to check on the work done and hear

Nirmala's complaints about the women. If they so much as opened their mouths in their own defence or against Nirmala, he would shut them up and threaten to have every one of them produced before the Superintendent on charges of misbehaviour. Only the Mate would be heard, no one else.

All of us decided to boycott Nirmala until she came to her senses. We also boycotted the matron, Swaran Kaur. These two had become great friends, and would lie on a cot in an empty cell giggling and gossiping all day. Their response to the boycott was defiant at first, and the ward was tense with hostility and fear because the prisoners suspected that the two women were plotting all kinds of conspiracies against them. But as the boycott drew on, both began to feel their isolation, especially when it became clear that Mr Singh was only exploiting them for her own ends. But that took almost two months.

Meanwhile we decided to talk to the new DSP and demand that Mrs Singh be controlled or else removed from the ward. He heard us out, but said finally that he was only in charge of us detenus; he could assure us that we ourselves would have nothing to complain about, but the women were in Mrs Singh's charge and only the Superintendent could do anything about that. He promised to bring the latter to the ward so that we could speak to him ourselves.

The Superintendent came next day with a retinue of officers and warders, stood nervously through our long report of the situation and asked the DSP to investigate the matter. The DSP refused point blank—it was not his responsibility, he said. The Superintendent, even more flustered by this, promised that he would look into the matter and hurried out.

Next morning we sent a written report cataloguing Mrs Singh's activities, demanding that the Superintendent make a personal enquiry on the spot and that he talk to all the female prisoners, not just to the matrons, *Numberdarni* and Mate. We urged him to remove Mrs Singh from her charge of the ward and restore the normal rights of the women immediately.

A week passed with no response from the Superintendent. On Saturday 3 April, things came dramatically to a head. Mrs Singh sent for Phoolmati at about 2.45 p.m. The girl was escorted out, shaking with terror, by the matron Swaran Kaur. Half an hour later we heard her screaming outside the ward and the matron's voice shouting at her to be quiet. We rushed out of our room just as she was pushed through the door where she fell in a heap on the ground, screaming and beating her face and breast. When she saw us she got up on her knees and with tears streaming down her face, breathless with hysteria and terror, she told us that she had been beaten all over her head and shoulders with Mrs Singh's boots and that the Matron had stuffed her mouth with her *chadder* or veil to stifle her screams. They had locked the door into Mrs Singh's office, fallen upon the girl and beaten her so savagely that she thought they would kill her.

The women gathered round, their faces pale with fear, and began to cry. For us, this was the last straw. We told the matrons to bring the Superintendent to the ward without delay. The Head Warder, hearing the commotion, rushed in and tried to calm us down. We turned on him and told him that if the Superintendent did not come at once there would be a riot in the ward. Just then a male prisoner accompanied by a warder brought in our tea. I went to the door and told them to take it back. We were on hunger strike and would take no food till the lunatic who had been given charge of this ward was thrown out. We had forewarned our fellow detenus that food returned would be the signal for a hunger strike. Seeing that we meant business, the Head Warder rushed out and came back in a few minutes with the DSP.

He was very quiet and listened without a murmur to our angry accusations. Would we have to wait for them to carry the dead bodies of these women out of here before they took action against Mrs Singh? we asked him. Then he made Phoolmati tell him what had happened. She did, showing the cuts and swellings on her head and shoulders where she had been beaten.

"*Dipty Sahib*," she begged, stretching her folded hands in supplication to him, "shoot me here right now, but don't let this woman murder me."

He was shaken and upset but tried to calm us down and said he would call the doctor to see Phoolmati at once.

The Doctor came, injected Phoolmati with glucose and said she must be hospitalised at once. But we were no longer going to be stalled and put off with soothing assurances that all would be looked into. The women declared that they too would go on hunger strike and not eat or work until Mrs Singh was removed from the ward. The DSP was worried because he knew that the other detenus, and perhaps the entire prison, would support us on this issue. He begged us to be patient; the Superintendent was not there at the moment but he would report the whole incident to him and bring him to the ward as soon as he returned.

At ten that night the Superintendent came to see us. First he went to the main barrack and assured the women that he would remove Mrs Singh from her charge over them. He urged them to eat their food, there was nothing more to worry about. Then he came to us.

"She is a sadist," he said, shaking his head. "I will not tolerate such inhuman behaviour. Please rest assured that she will be removed tomorrow. Only please take your meal now, I give you my word that the woman will be removed."

But for a whole week, though Mrs Singh kept well out of the way, nothing happened. So we threatened a hunger strike again and the women sent a written petition which all of them signed, demanding that the Superintendent keep his word and saying that they would not eat or work until he did.

Finally Mrs Singh was removed and an enquiry was ordered against her. But this was a mere formality. The enquiry petered out and the women only got real relief and all their rights restored to them when the entire female ward was transferred to Hissar some three or four weeks later.

No one dared to proceed against Mrs Singh, even though there was now no question of her resuming charge of the ward again. But until it became *de jure*, no other officer was willing to take charge of the women unless given full authority to do so. Mrs Singh, meanwhile, smarting under the "insult to her reputation", made a counter charge that we, the detenues, and the officers in charge of us, had incited the prisoners against her. The jail authorities even gave that some credence, but dropped the whole matter with relief when the ward was transferred to Hissar.

It was 'incitement' to tell the cruelly suffering prisoners to speak up for their rights. We had suffered with them and experienced the excruciatingly slow progress from dumb submission to faltering speech and finally, after a whole year, to a declaration of revolt. And yet we were accused of incitement. It was not considered incitement to perpetrate these crimes on the helpless prisoners. Of course, the same situation prevailed outside prison as well. And when the people cried halt, it was sufficient to claim that they were being 'incited' by 'mischievous' and 'anti-social' elements. What excuses will be found, I wondered, when the people, driven beyond endurance by these custodians of the law, are forced to revolt?

Since letters to friends and detenus in other jails were not permitted, I took to writing long letters in my journal to those I could not reach. In one such to Srilata, written about six months after my arrest, I had expressed my feelings about being cut off from the outside world:

"When this is over, the first person apart from my family I want to meet is you. The others have receded rather. They represent the onward moving world, having no relation to us, stilled, held still by these walls. I hope they are well and happy and that work goes on. But in relation to me, they have passed me over. They are living complete lives without me. I resent this a little at times, even as I realise that it must and should be this way. I mean, after a point we cease to exist except as a memory. We are tucked away, oh with affection and pride and respect, but out of the vividness of life. Yes, as though we were dead. And in a sense this is the real, the ultimate negation of being in prison. We *are* as dead. Outside, life flows on. We are part of a past life, a past time, when we too were alive and moving. . . ."

This is what I felt, and yet life in the ward could not have been more intense. The struggle to understand and unite the prisoners to resist Mrs Singh was, for me, a continuation of the struggle we had waged outside. A vital affirmation that wherever one is, wherever there are people, there is strife and struggle and life. The one thing I dreaded was being put into solitary confinement, and even that dread was overcome after the transfer to Hissar, when I burrowed deeper and deeper into my reading, jottings in my journal, and the thoughts which were spurred on by what I read and which I had the luxury of time to follow through to their conclusions.

My world outside was changing. Charles and Karoki left for England in April 1976, after a last desperate effort to get me released so that I could go with them. But the government was adamant. No way were they going to let me out even though they had just released Srilata quite suddenly on a month's parole. Then, just as she was getting ready to take the train back to Delhi and jail from Madras where her parents lived, a telegraphic message was received saying that she would be released on condition that she stayed within the limits of Madras city for the duration of the emergency. There was no restriction on her activities or movement within this area, and she soon began work in the CPI-led Dock Workers Union. It was a relief that Srilata was out, and the conditions imposed were not too onerous considering the continuing state of emergency. Srilata's grandmother had been a stalwart of the Congress during the freedom movement and was a close friend of the Nehru family. Well advanced in age, she had made a personal appeal to Mrs Gandhi to release Srilata on parole so that she could see her before she died.

With Charles and Karoki gone, the strain of my detention became more severe on my parents. As long as we were in Ambala it had been easy for them to drive from Chandigarh, which was only twenty miles away, and see me every week. These visits kept them in good cheer because they went back each time, reassured that I was in good health and spirits. Their real worry was not only that I had been detained because of personal spite and vengeance but that my detention would last indefinitely for the same reason. Both of them, especially my father, were getting on in years and he suffered from an asthmatic complaint which was exacerbated by the strain and anxiety caused by my detention.

The possibility that we might be sent to Hissar was a blow. Far away from Chandigarh, with very bad roads and no direct train connections, my parents could only get there by country bus, and it would be necessary to find a place to stay overnight as the journey was too long to be able to return the same day. They had no friends in Hissar who could put them up, and the only hotels in the place were seedy dens and quite unsuitable for them.

I wrote to the Delhi Administration requesting permission to remain in Ambala on compassionate grounds, and pointed out that as facilities for detenus were supposed to have no connection with the other prisoners, it would be no inconvenience to the jail authorities to keep me there as the female ward would continue to be used for undertrial prisoners. Kamla, too, was anxious to stay in Ambala because her family lived in Yamuna-nagar, which was almost as close as Chandigarh, but Hissar was off the route altogether and they would have an even harder time getting there than my family. Pushpa did not mind the move as it would make only a marginal difference to her family in Delhi.

Our appeals were ignored and we did not get so much as a reply. Actually we suspected that the jail authorities wanted us out of the way to avoid any more trouble with Mrs Singh, and might well have initiated the move themselves.

The Borstal Institution and Juvenile Jail in Hissar, it was claimed, was the most modern and well equipped jail in the country. It had been built along the lines of some Australian institution—an 'open' jail and the foremost of its kind in Asia. Just completed, it had a wing which was to be the Central Jail for Women in Haryana and we were going to be its first incumbents. We heard from officers and warders who had been there that there were flush toilets in every cell, beds for the prisoners and special interview rooms for them so that they could meet their visitors in comfort.

The female convicts left in May 1976. It was a tearful parting as there was no certainty at the time that we would be transfer-red there as well. A few weeks later, Kamla got her transfer orders from the Haryana government, and again there was no knowing whether Pushpa and I, who were under the jurisdiction of the Delhi Administration, would also be sent. Another ten days went by and then on the 9th of June we got our orders to move to Hissar as well.

I was in the middle of an interview with my parents when the order was delivered. They took it well, although this would put me effectively out of their reach. But we were grateful that we had this chance to see each other and to say goodbye.

Pushpa and I left for Hissar next morning with another detenu, Dharam Singh Rathi, after waiting for him in the office for two hours because, we were told, he had insisted on having *kheer*, a kind of rice pudding, cooked for him before he would leave. He appeared at last, an old man, well over seventy years of age, almost blind with cataract, groping his way forward with a stick. But he had a voice like a trumpet and was surprisingly bold, relaxed and humorous. A top-ranking leader of the BLD in Haryana, he was one of Bansilal's chief and most vociferous opponents, and was being transferred to the District Jail in Rohtak where most of the opposition VIPs were detained.

The police escort consisted of three policewomen, four armed constables and an ASI carrying a gleaming pistol. This latter was Rati Singh, an immaculately uniformed, quick-witted, eagle-eyed young man with a biting sense of humour. We launched into a political discussion almost immediately, initiated by the ASI Rati Singh. He wanted to know what we thought we were achieving by remaining inside. Outside everyone was indifferent, and the opposition, especially in Haryana, was in a flux of defections to the ruling Congress Party. He took delight in naming some of the big guns who had recently changed sides, provoking old Dharam Singh Rathi to boom out his derision at all such scum. Pushpa and I maintained that if people outside were indifferent to our fate it was only a reflection of our own failure and we could not blame them. The opposition had spent all its time chasing votes and seats, and had never given the people and their needs a thought. The old man agreed, but defended himself by saying that our people had slavery and acquiescence in their very blood and bones. They would never rise up. They had taken invasion after invasion, enslavement after enslavement lying down through the centuries and were beyond hope.

Then he took another tack. The only man, he said, who could down Mrs Gandhi was Bansilal himself. He would do this through the defence forces. But the way he would do it, having already alienated the *Sikh*s, who made up a large section of the army, by replacing *Sikh* officers with *Jats*, would bring about a civil war which was the only solution to the problems of the country.

I was struck by the gap between professional politicians like Rathi and people like myself. The politician sees only the manipulation and intrigue of the *durbar* as real. He has no faith in the people and is interested in them only as a statistic, or a crowd to compel and exploit for his own ends. Even when he is not dishonest or corrupt or selfish, he acts only from above, from within the power elite. The masses of the people below exist only to be acted upon, not as a force to be motivated into action for their own interests. The politician does not dare to risk that for fear of losing his leadership.

But Dharam Singh Rathi was an impressive man. Old, frail, and nearly blind as he was, he had been cruelly humiliated by Bansilal before his arrest. The policewomen told us in a whisper that his hair had been shaved off, and he had been paraded through the streets of his constituency town. Yet here he was, full of verve and fire, quite relaxed and without malice or resentment at his maltreatment by the government. He and Rati Singh kept up a lively dialogue of political gossip while the rest of us listened quietly in amusement. Pushpa and I kept our eyes on the windows of the van, looking curiously at the scene outside, the sights and sounds of a world that we seemed to have left behind forever.

It was fiercely hot till we branched off the main Delhi-Ambala highway at Panipat. Then it suddenly clouded over, rained hard and the rest of the journey was beautifully cool. We had to stop for lunch, and I pleaded that we find a green spot outside the towns where we could eat the packed lunch which had been prepared for us by our fellow detenus in Ambala, who had sent it to the ward with affectionate farewell messages for us. The police had food with them too, so we agreed to have a picnic lunch by the grassy banks of a canal down which we women strolled while the men stopped for tea at a roadside tea shop.

We spent an hour in the open, stretching our legs, breathing the fresh air and savouring the wonder of seeing no walls or barriers around us after a full year.

About two hours later we reached Rohtak. We were amused to see the huge, grotesquely painted pictures of Indira and Sanjay Gandhi at street crossings and on walls all over the market place. There were also portraits of Nehru and Mahatma Gandhi, and posters with slogans about the 20-Point Programme and calls for discipline and hard work everywhere. At one *chowk* or square, there was a portrait of the Mahatma with a quotation below it which read "The India of my Dreams". Just above this was a lurid advertisement for a film called *Charas* (marijuana).

Pushpa and I laughed at the piquancy of it.

When we reached the jail we found that they had received no message that Rathi was being sent there, and the jailor refused to take him in even though he had his transfer orders with him. It took over two hours and summoning the CID before he was let in. We wondered if we would have the same trouble in Hissar which we reached just before dark. The jail was at the other end of the town and we came upon it suddenly, its red brick walls rising starkly from the green fields which surrounded it.

Once again the great iron gates opened to let us in and then shut behind us. But now we felt quite at home in prison. There was no officer on duty, and while we waited for him to come and register us in we studied our surroundings. The inner gate had a peep hole through which I had a quick look and saw a huge playing field. The board in the hall stated that there were 150 inmates in the jail and three detenus under MISA. We wondered who the other two could be. Then we saw that the entrance to the female ward was just to the right of the main entrance. We put our eyes to the crack between the doors and caught a glimpse of Kamla sitting in the corridor with Sita, who had also been transferred here from Ambala. We banged on the door and shouted to them and they came running out. They were not expecting us and our delight at being together again was all the greater because Kamla had given up hope of our coming after ten days had passed with no news of our transfer.

The DSP arrived. He had been in charge of us in Ambala before being posted here, and we greeted each other like old friends. ASI Rati Singh having handed us over, now took his leave of us, and after being registered we were taken into the ward by Kamla and Sita.

Inside there was bedlam. The women had been locked up for the night, and having heard that we had arrived were straining against the bars and yelling for us to come to them. They demanded to be let out so that we could greet each other properly, but the matron said she would let us into their barrack rather than let them out. It was a noisy and boisterous reunion. We were pulled and grabbed from all sides with each one wanting to show us the wonders of their new habitation.

"Look *Didi*, look, we have proper beds with *durrees* on them!"

"Look, there is a seperate *ghara* for each of us and each has its own stand!"

"*Didi*, come and see the bathrooms—there are mirrors, wash basins and water in the lavatories!"

At last we bade them good night and went into Kamla's room. Here again, the office of the yet-to-be-appointed Lady Assistant Jail Superintendent had been made over to her, and we sat down on her bed feeling quite stunned that we were together again.

Kamla told us that this jail was very relaxed, everyone was anxious to make up to the women for the experience they had undergone with Mrs Singh in Ambala, and were out to be kind and permissive. But the lack of discipline was having an adverse effect on the prisoners, who had started to quarrel bitterly among themselves and had become quite uncontrollable. Kamla said they had been unable to digest their new-found freedom and were running riot as a result. The amity and solidarity that had been achieved with such difficulty in Ambala had evaporated and not a day passed without a violent and noisy quarrel. The women had split up into two camps, one consisting of the short-term convicts and the other of lifers. Phoolmati and Maya were the main targets of hostility, and they maintained it was because the others were jealous of the 'gifts' we were supposed to have given them before they left Ambala. Kamla said that the place was like a madhouse echoing with their quarrels, and she had been made utterly miserable by their inconsiderate and noisy behaviour.

We would tackle all these problems together now and, deeply grateful that we were together again, we pulled our cots out into the little yard next to Kamla's room and fell asleep long after midnight.

At 5 a.m. we were awakened by the Head Warder, a scrawny ancient with what seemed like just one long tooth in his mouth, clumping by with his stick, banging on the floor and wishing us *namaste* as he passed on his way down the corridor to open up the cells and let the prisoners out. While we waited for Phoolmati to make tea, Kamla showed us round the ward. A long, narrow corridor ran down the length of the ward between blocks of barred cells and barracks, with an open courtyard between each block. There were three of these courtyards, the largest as big as a badminton court, open to the sky and surrounded by high brick walls.

Not a bird, nor a leaf nor a blade of grass could be seen. Not
a sound but the raucous voices of the inmates which echoed from
end to end. It was like being sealed up in a capsule or shut up in
a glorified cattle shed. Pushpa and I were struck dumb by the
contrast of this place with Ambala. This was a real jail, prison
as I had always dreaded it; bleak, grim and sterile, a place where
the soul would dry up for lack of the sustaining nourishment of
sun and shade, trees and bird life and space. That square acre in
Ambala, filled with the quite beauty of an *ashram* had afforded
the eye a perspective, a horizon, a harmony which had brought
peace and given comfort through all the distractions and tensions
of our time there.

And this place was the pride of the prison bureaucracy of
Haryana! How stupid, unimaginative this modern architecture
was. Imported from Australia, where conditions of climate and
society were quite different, this was another of those transplants
which were totally unsuited to our conditions and our needs. The
building was also typical of all such construction in the country.
In this brand new jail, just opened with so much fanfare, the walls
were already damp, their plaster peeling and cracking. The
floors, crudely finished, were also cracked, the lavatories did not
flush and were lying choked up and stinking; the electricity
switches did not work, and there wasn't so much as a nail or rack
for the prisoners to put their clothes and belongings on. The
contractors had done their job as usual, using shoddy material,
undercutting both on quantity and on quality, making huge profits and buying off the authorities responsible for giving them
completion certificates.

Kamla took our outraged protests calmly. She had spent ten
terrible days here already; the heat and dust and noise had driven
her mad to start with, but then she had adjusted to the place. She
realised that this was going to be her 'home' for a long time to
come and whenever she was arrested again, since she was a
local resident and this was the central jail for women in Haryana.
We would get used to it too, she told us placidly, just give it time.
We were shocked by her resignation and decided to write at
once to the authorities complaining that our being put into a
place like this was punitive rather than preventive detention and
against MISA regulations. We demanded that we and all the
female prisoners be allowed to use the open grounds outside the

ward for at least an hour every day or we would all suffocate
inside. This sports ground was only for the use of the boys in the
Borstal section, and was out of bounds for the women who were
confined to the ward. Of course our protests and appeals had no
effect, and we soon got used to our surroundings as Kamla had
said we would.

The cells for solitary confinement were at the far end of the
corridor, and two of these were inhabited by two MISA detenues
from Pakistan who had been arrested in Jammu. They were two
old women and appeared to be in a most miserable condition of
neglect and isolation—a situation which we were able to change
gradually. I opted to take a cell opposite them as this would give
me some privacy and it was at a distance from the main barrack
so that there was less noise here. Pushpa and Kamla would share
the office, next to which was the matron's room which had been
turned over to us for use as a kitchen. As we were the only detenus here, we would have our own kitchen and Phoolmati and
Maya would do our cooking for us.

So we settled in, but the first task that faced us was to bring
peace to the female ward rent by the quarrels of the women
who, with no Mrs Singh to terrorise them, had allowed their
pent-up frustrations to burst out, and no one seemed able to
restore order or keep control any longer.

As I understood it, our task was to make the prisoners realise
that their salvation lay in solidarity alone, whether in the face
of an external threat like Mrs Singh or that of their own selfishness, opportunism, and malice which only set one against the
other in mistrust, competition, and envy, destroying all chance
of their making any positive use of their time in jail.

In Hissar there was no external threat. In fact the laxity of
the jail authorities had the effect of intensifying the quarrels and
vendettas of the women in defiance of all remonstrance. Sita,
the senior matron, took refuge in simply withdrawing from and
ignoring the problem, and the other matron, a new recruit called
Manju, was too raw and young to exercise her authority without
Sita's backing. The old Head Warder was kindly but ineffectual
with his long-winded exhortations for peace and the officers
told us that they were unused to handling women convicts and

that until the lady assistant jailor was appointed they hoped that we would take care of the problems in the ward. They said that they knew of only one way to keep order, and that was the stick. This they felt was too harsh a measure to use against the women and they knew of no other.

The result was that there was a vacuum of authority in the ward. We detenues could exert only a moral influence on the prisoners, having no legal authority, while everyone else just passed the buck.

The situation in the ward became intolerable. As I mentioned earlier, the trouble seemed to have started in a quarrel between the short and long term prisoners. On further investigation it appeared that when they had first arrived in Hissar their unity and goodwill had been unalloyed. Then a problem arose about their accommodation in the main barrack, which was divided into two sections with a small yard in between, and some twelve beds in each section. They had all wanted to be together, but there wasn't room for all of them and they had to spilt up. After prolonged debate, Nirmala decided that the best way was to put the lifers in one section and the short term convicts in the other. She clinched the matter with the Head Warder without consulting the other prisoners. This was taken as a breach of faith, a deliberate move on the part of the lifers to segregate themselves from the others.

Feelings were particularly bitter because whereas it is the normal tendency in prison for the lifer to lord it over the others, in the struggle against Mrs Singh in Ambala such differences had been obliterated; all the short-term prisoners had stood by the lifers and backed them steadfastly. Now they were not prepared to lose their hard-won equality with the *dadas* or bullyboys of the ward.

Instead of discussing and sorting out the misunderstanding, both sides took the offensive, picked quarrels with one another and tried to get each other into trouble by fabricating reports, carrying tales and complaining about one another to the warders, matrons and even the officers at the slightest opportunity. The officers, who had started out with considerable goodwill for the prisoners because of their experience at the hands of the notorious Mrs Singh, soon began to lose patience and we detenues realised that if the jail staff were pressed much further the situation would quickly deteriorate as it had in Ambala.

We warned the women about this and tried to make them see that they were jeopardising their own best interests by their inopportune and intemperate behaviour. Our remedy was to suggest a weekly *panchayat* where everyone would have the opportunity to air their views and grievances and where decisions could be taken collectively. No charges or accusations should be made without proper investigation, and if all this was done openly and in front of everyone there would be less room for the kind of wild charges, denials and covering-up of facts being bandied about now. We wanted the *panchayat* to be attended by the entire ward, including the matron on duty, so that no one could say she had not been consulted or try to evade responsibility for decisions collectively reached.

We discussed this proposal with the matrons and the officer in charge of the ward. They welcomed it but were sceptical of its success. Then we talked to each prisoner individually. All of them agreed to give it a try although some who were less than enthusiastic, thought that while the idea was a good one they were all too stubborn, selfish, and short-sighted to see what was good for them.

"You have done a lot for us, now don't bother yourselves any more for us, we're not worth the trouble. You will never find the head nor the tail to our fights. Leave us to ourselves, we are a bad lot."

We told them that this was impossible. We were living in the same ward, and we could not help but be affected by what went on. It was our common responsibility to create a peaceful and friendly atmosphere in which all of us could live. We warned them that their quarrels, petty complaints and unruly behaviour would lose them the officers' goodwill and that this would harm all of them. We also pointed out that we detenues, Kamla, Pushpa and I, found the din of quarrel and strife they raised all day intolerable, and some way must be found to put a stop to it.

So the first meeting was held one afternoon, and a number of issues were thrashed out. The trouble caused by the gifts we were supposed to have given Maya and Phoolmati was discussed. When the women were leaving Ambala the three of us had fished around our all too few belongings to see what we could distribute to the most needy in the way of clothes, shoes, plastic containers, combs, toothbrushes, etc. Maya and Phoolmati got no more than anyone else, although in fact they deserved it for all the help they had given us.

The women declared themselves satisfied, and told us that they were not hungry for things but for love. They felt that we were biased in favour of Maya and Phoolmati, and accused the two of them of exploiting this bias. We explained that although at a personal level we undoubtedly felt closer to Maya and Phoolmati because of all they had done for us, even at risk to themselves, and because of our closer contact with them in the past year, we were sure they could not point to a single instance when we had favoured them in any way over the others, or exercised our influence with the officers exclusively in their favour. However, if Maya and Phoolmati were using their friendship with us to lord it over the others in any way, this was obviously very wrong. The two girls denied that they had done any such thing. They said that they knew very well how offensive such behaviour would be to us, and that it was quite clear that we regarded all the prisoners with the same feelings. They said that these accusations were just a manifestation of the endemic jealousy and suspicion they felt towards each other, and it was wrong to drag us into it. The others seemed to accept this and we moved on to the next issue.

The next problem was that of the *langar* or kitchen. This had caused bitter quarrels from the day of its inception, although it was by choice that the women had been allowed to run their own kitchen in the ward. Three long-term convicts had been selected to run it. This was arranged by Kamla and the matrons in consultation with the women, not only to try and heal the rift between them, but also because kitchen workers were entitled to the most remission and the highest pay, and it was generally the long term prisoners who were selected to do this work.

The chance to run their own kitchen could have been a boon for everyone in the ward if they had cooperated in the task; tea-making and the chance to introduce some small variety in the dreary daily diet could have been facilitated. Instead, the kitchen staff simply aroused the envy, suspicion and hostility of the other prisoners who accused them of stealing supplies, bribing the matrons, helping themselves to the rations and shortchanging the others. A running quarrel ensued, with the prisoners hanging around the kitchen, spying on the women inside and provoking them in turn into stormy scenes when they would refuse to work and insist that the others either stop accusing them or do the work themselves.

After some heated discussion it was accepted that the *langar* work would be rotated every three months so that everyone would get a chance. Meanwhile there was to be no more hanging about the kitchen and prying. Any complaints or suspicions could be voiced to the matrons or the *Numberdarni*, who would investigate them and the matter could be thrashed out in the *panchayat*. If the kitchen staff did make themselves an extra cup of tea now and then this was only reasonable, and as long as they used their own supplies of tea and sugar no one should mind. Finally it was agreed that on no account would any complaints be made to the officers unless a decision to do so was taken in the *panchayat*.

The meeting broke up after some three hours when Pushpa, Kamla and I retired to our room for a cup of tea. We were fairly satisfied with the way things had gone; if this method of holding a *panchayat* every week was sustained, it would gradually develop understanding and cooperation between the prisoners. We were joined by Sita, Maya, and Phoolmati. They said we were dreamers if we thought that the *panchayat* had solved anything. The women were too perverse to see what was in their best interests, and we should not expect anything from this initiative. We told them that while we saw that no sudden change could be expected, the way of the *panchayat* was the only one that could solve our problems and we felt duty bound to persist in our efforts to make it work.

There was peace in the ward for several days after the meeting, but then the atmosphere became tense again. We ignored the whispering and talk around us, determined to implement the decision to bring all complaints to the *panchayat*. When the day came we waited for the women to call the meeting at the appointed time. No one moved. Instead, choosing just that moment, Dhanni and Nirmala, who were both working in the prisoners' kitchen, demanded to be taken to see the officer in charge. Maya and Phoolmati came to us full of anxiety, insisting that the two were going to make some complaint about them.

"You think they are interested in the *panchayat?* They are

doing this just to spite you. They can't stand the fact that we share your food and are closer to you than they are. They've sworn that they'll get us both into trouble somehow or other, and now they're going to fabricate some complaint and put us to shame before the officers."

We could not believe this. Dhanni and Nirmala might have some quite legitimate complaint to make about supplies to the *langar*.

"Why didn't they wait and bring it up at the *panchayat?*" Maya demanded. "That's what we decided last week."

We explained to her that confidence in the *panchayat* could not be forced on the women. This would develop once they realised that it was the only way to solve their problems. As for their demand to see the officers, the girls had nothing to worry about if they had done no wrong. We should wait and see what happened.

Dhanni and Nirmala returned in a few minutes looking very pleased with themselves, and passed by without a look in our direction. The matron announced that the officer now wanted to see Phoolmati and Maya. They were in such a panic, we had to push them out of the ward. When they came back they told us that it was just as they had suspected. Dhanni and Nirmala had complained that they were quarrelsome and created trouble in the ward. The officer had asked the matron if this was true, and she had said that she had never found this to be the case. He had then told the girls that all the prisoners should learn to live peacefully together, and sent them back without saying more.

We felt that nothing had been lost, but Phoolmati and Maya were very upset.

"Don't you see?" Phoolmati said, "this is the way we lose the respect and goodwill of the officers. This is how we cut our own throats. God! I'm a lifer and once the officers turn hostile a lifer has no chance."

Everyone realised that this had been a violation of the agreement that no one would complain to the authorities about any prisoner until the matter had been discussed in the *panchayat*. Feeling guilty and somewhat defensive, the two truants tried to deny that they had made any complaints about the two girls, saying that they had only reported the lack of proper supplies to the *langar*. Guilt kept things quiet for a while and then there was another blow-up, followed by two or three days of intense and hysterical quarrelling, after which peace was restored again quite suddenly. And so it went on. It was quite beyond our understanding; these quarrels had no logic or cause that we could identify; and the bitterness and venom they generated was exhausting even to observe, yet just as suddenly as they erupted they would die down. When their blood was up it seemed that the women had a desperate, perverse determination to bring down a holocaust upon themselves.

We tried every way we knew to make them see reason, but then they turned against us too. Who were we, MISA-*wallis*, to interfere? They even accused us of turning the officers against them. Their malice towards us was unnerving and we realised that we still had a lot to learn about their psychology.

So far we had regarded the prisoners as more sinned against than sinning, victims of a society that forced them into crime. But we had failed to understand that they too had become corrupted in the process. We had recognised the extent of their frustration and insecurity under the deprivations and constraints of prison life. One day, in a poignantly reflective mood, Nirmala said, "*Didi*, how can I endure these twenty years in here? You don't know what it's like. Death is better than this slavery."

For the first time I realised what prison meant to the convict, especially to the lifer. We detenus, with our political consciousness and convictions, had resources which these prisoners did not have. Moreover, life for us was easy compared with theirs. We were treated with respect and we could exercise our right to be treated as human beings. We had the status of our class and education, and we had material facilities of accommodation and food commensurate with our status.

These prisoners had nothing. They were subject to the mercy of the jail gods. They had no 'right' to their rights. Jail rules were dependant on the goodwill of the authorities, and the exercise of duty, the implementation of rules, enmeshed in a web of fear and favour, ould never be taken for granted.

What was unknown here was that conscious interrelation of rights and responsibilities which constitutes the only disciplined and principled basis of human existence. To my mind the absence of this dimension constitutes degradation. And this dimension was conspicuous by its absence, not only in the relations between the prisoners and the jail authorities, but in the relations between the lower and higher ranks of the latter as well. Doubtless it is ultimately a socio-political phenomenon—the effect of a feudal-authoritarian society where there is no real democratic spirit or consciousness. In this sense prison was merely a microcosm of life outside. The struggle in Mehrauli had been basically about this. But the fact that these relations degrade and corrupt both or all the parties concerned cannot be ignored. Otherwise there is danger of idealisation and falsification, which can lead one to make serious mistakes in one's attempts to change the situation.

For change it must. But the mistake we made was to confuse the conditions of life of these prisoners with the conditions of life of the poor and oppressed outside. I, in particular, tried to use the same methods here as I had learned to use in my work among the *purabias* of Mehrauli. There were similarities of course. For example, the venom and bitterness of the infighting among the prisoners reminded me of the *purabias*, festering under the daily humiliations of their existence but ready to defend their "name" and honour at knifepoint over the pettiest issues among themselves.

While it was clear that for both the *purabias* and the prisoners the ultimate release lay in unity and resistance against oppression, the options open to those outside prison were far more and far more varied than for those inside. At worst those outside could retreat and go away, at best they could choose their own ground and weapons; but here, behind stone walls and bars, this was not possible.

Apart from the physical constraints, there were also the effects of prison life on moral and spiritual values. In prison the convict —and also the political prisoner to some extent—is trapped in a totally exposed and public situation. There is no escape from others. Privacy is inconceivable. Torn from your family and loved ones, you are thrown into a hostile and exposed situation where you must even grieve in public. In order to survive, you learn the

way of subterfuge and lies. Every few days the tension that builds
up inside you bursts in a fury of aggressive frustration. Blindly
you attack the very ones who can help you and share your grief.
And even as you rage and fight you are gripped with the fear that
if caught, you will land yourself in trouble, perhaps have your
ticket blotted. And so you learn to cover up, to lie blandly, and
to project an innocence which belies the savagery that wells up
inside you. You slyly put the blame on others, carrying tales and
whispering reports in order to confuse and blur the picture. And
finally you end up at a point when you can no longer distinguish
truth from falsehood, reality from illusion and love from hate.

The tensions, frustrations and hysteria that burst into the
open at Hissar after being contained for so long in Ambala under
Mrs Singh's reign of terror, revealed the women convicts in a
new light. They were at the mercy of passions which we had not
recognised so far. We had to find new ways to get through
to them. Our attempts to deal with them collectively were
perhaps premature. We should have tried to build up friendship
and trust before thinking about solidarity. To start with, however, we would have to administer some kind of shock treatment
to shake them out of the madness which had gripped them and
had caused them to turn on us as well.

We wanted to make them see that by turning on us they were
hurting and possibly even losing real friends. We decided to with-
draw from all contact with them, to go about our own business
and to ignore them as completely as possible. When they realised
that we had stopped talking to them and expressing our concern
for them, their first reaction was one of defiance. To hell with
us, they could look after themselves. They used to snigger and
pass sniping remarks when we took our solemn walks up and
down the corridor after meals. Then they tried to provoke us to
respond, even in anger, but although they managed to trap
Pushpa into conversation sometimes, we held fast to our decision
and waited for them to figure out why we were 'boycotting'
them.

In Ambala this method of boycott had been used very effectively against Nirmala. It was only after she realised and admitted
her mistake in agreeing to become Mate and Mrs Singh's
stooge, that she was admitted back into the fold. We had agreed
then that this method would be used against all those who persis-

tently betrayed the interests of the ward. So the prisoners were aware of what we were doing, and we left it to them to take the initiative in restoring normal relations.

September 1976 was the most difficult month of my entire detention. The hostile surroundings of the jail itself were compounded by the sadness of seeing my parents looking old, frail and exhausted by the long and uncomfortable journey from Chandigarh to Hissar on their first visit to me since our meeting in Ambala on 9 July. It was in this month too that the tension and strife in the ward had reached a peak with the convicts turning hostile towards us. And it was in this month that Kamla left us for medical treatment in Rohtak. Her health had deteriorated badly and she was in continuous pain now. After eight months the doctors had finally diagnosed her trouble. It was cervical spondilitus and she would have to be hospitalised for traction and proper treatment. She would also have to wear a collar round her neck.

Although we had been demanding for months that she be X-rayed and given a thorough check-up, and though the jail authorities had done their best to get permission for her transfer to the medical college in Rohtak, the only place where there were facilities available for her treatment, there had been no response from the government. It was only when the Civil Surgeon of Hissar sent an urgent wire to the government that she must be transferred immediately, that orders were at last passed for her removal to Rohtak.

Kamla bore her pain with great fortitude. She had to stop all games and exercise except for walking slowly and doing some special neck and facial exercises. She found it increasingly difficult to read and write for any length of time, and some nights she could not sleep for the pain. At times she was in such agony that we could only weep to see her struggle with the pain. Yet she never complained. She was full of fun and humour the moment the worst attacks passed, always ready for a laugh, full of tenderness, affection and concern, longing for the serious discussions and study with Pushpa and me which she found impossible to cope with as the attacks of pain grew in severity and frequency.

The parting was sad and filled us with anxiety. There was no knowing what would happen and when we might meet again. The uncertainty of the future, and our fear that she would be alone with none of us to nurse her, made us even more miserable.

I missed Kamla more than I had thought possible. She was the one person with whom I could be myself. We had learned a great deal from each other and were able to encourage and cheer one another in those times of sadness and depression when comradely strength of mind and conviction help to stand one on one's feet.

Another cause for depression and concern, even before Kamla left, was the uncertainty and irregularity of our correspondence with our families. In Ambala there had never been any trouble on this count. Letters to and from the detenus had been despatched and delivered promptly. But in Hissar not only were we unable to meet our families for long intervals but our letters were either held up or lost, causing anxiety and strain all round. The jail authorities insisted that the fault was not theirs and blamed the CID men (who censored all letters) for the delays. We sent letters of complaint to the government, the police, the post office, and the higher jail authorities, but to no effect. Letters could take anything from fifteen days to a month to arrive, and that too if they arrived at all. Later we learned from an underground pamphlet send to us that Hissar jails (the older District jail housed the adult male prisoners and lots of male detenus as well) were notorious for this harassment of detenus, not only with their letters but in their interviews with their relatives as well.

The final blow in this series of depressing events was the quarrel with Maya. So far, although we had not exempted Phoolmati and Maya from the misdoings of the prisoners as a whole, they had, by virtue of the fact that they worked for us, been more sensible and rational than the others. Phoolmati was given to great instability and hysteria, but even she was able to see where she had gone wrong once the fit was over. Maya, on the other hand, had always been one of the most solid and dependable of the women in the ward.

After Kamla's departure for Rohtak, we were told that we should now release one of the girls as there wasn't enough work for both. This was quite true, as I did my own work anyway and most of the work had been created by Kamla's illness. As Phoolmati was far away from her village and her people could not afford to visit her more than once or twice a year, she needed more than Maya, the facilities we could share with her, as the latter's village was very close to Hissar and she was visited by her relatives every week or ten days.

Moreover, Phoolmati was a lifer and in greater need of the remissions and higher pay she got by working in our kitchen, whereas Maya, after an appeal in the high Court, had recently had her life sentence commuted to five years. Four of these had already been served so that she would be going home in under a year now. All this considered, Pushpa and I felt that it was only fair to keep Phoolmati on and to release Maya for some other work.

We discussed the matter with the two of them, explaining why we felt that Phoolmati should be the one to stay on with us, and were relieved to see that both girls responded sensibly and accepted the choice without hard feelings. But as soon as word got around the ward that Maya was being released, the rest of the women, and especially Dhanni and Nirmala, rounded on her, jeering at the way she had been summarily "kicked out". They told her that we had enough "power" to have kept both of them on had we wanted, and said that it was Santosh who had poisoned us against her and influenced us to throw her out.

Instead of reacting with her usual good sense, Maya lost her balance and became hostile towards us as well. She insisted that Phoolmati had poisoned us against her, and nothing we could say would convince her otherwise. At last, outraged and exhausted at the intransigence and unreason of the girl, Puspha and I asked her to go away and leave us alone. It really was the last straw.

The accumulated effect of all this resulted in my going down with a short but painful attack of fever which was, however, promptly treated by the doctor, and with Pushpa's excellent nursing I was soon back on my feet. But after this I retreated almost totally into myself. I needed to revive the springs of my own resources and to restore the balance and stability which, to some extent, I had lost since coming to Hissar. I had to come to terms with a situation which I found bleak and hostile in every respect.

I began to read seriously, making notes and keeping a journal once again. I listened to music on my transistor and walked in the small yard behind my cell which was the only part of the ward where I could be alone. I watched the clouds and the sky, catching a glimpse of birds flying above, and listening to the call of peacocks from the fields behind the walls. Slowly I felt reason and peace flow back, and in a month I was myself again—albeit sadder and a little wiser perhaps.

I would like to say something more about Pushpa Kale. A tiny, sprightly woman of forty-two, mother of two sons and a daughter, Pushpa was a Maharashtrian from a coastal village in western India a short distance from the city of Bombay. The Kale family had settled in Delhi more than twenty years ago, and Vasant Rao Kale, Pushpa's husband, was a real estate agent who ran his own business. Pushpa was an active political worker for the Jan Sangh, and like Kamla she had an RSS background.

Puspha was a tireless worker, and whether it was nursing someone who was sick, bandaging an injury, cooking for people, knitting, or teaching the prisoners, she was busy night and day, practical and charitable above all. Her kindliness and devotion to what she saw as her religious duty was unquestionable.

A Brahmin by caste, she was religious in a very different way from Kamla. She observed all the brahminical rituals of prayer, fasting, purification and charity, and held certain beliefs and superstitions which Kamla and I questioned. But although we often argued with her about these, we were unable to make the least dent in her convictions. Apart from this, however, she was quite free of casteism and brahminical fastidiousness in practice as her unhesitating initiative in helping anyone in need, irrespective of their caste or creed, proved time and again. She was also a very warm and kind person, and excellent company in the grim prison surroundings.

So far I have commented only in passing on the life of the warders and matrons in the jail, and most of my comments have been negative. To set the record straight I must write a little more about how their job conditions affected them.

During the emergency all leave for jail staff was cancelled, and the warders and matrons were on call twenty-four hours a day

seven days a week. With salaries ranging from Rs 200 per month
for junior staff to a little over Rs 350 for senior people with 20
years or more service to their credit, it was not surprising that
they fell victim to the corruption which was rampant in the jails.
They were frank about the bribes they took in order to supple-
ment their meagre incomes, and justified this by saying that what
they took was nothing compared to the extortion at higher levels,
i.e., by the officers.

The warders' lives were hardly different in essence from those
of the prisoners. Confined to the jail premises while on duty, they
were also forced to do domestic work in the officers' houses
during their time off. Although this was strictly against the rules
of service none of them dared refuse, and although they were not
paid for this work, they did get some fringe benefits like a cup
of tea, free vegetables from the jail farms, and above all, the
'goodwill' of the officers for whom they worked.

One night in Hissar, when Phoolmati and Maya were washing
up after dinner and the Head Warder was waiting for them to
finish so that he could lock them up and sign out for the night,
Kamla, Pushpa and I had a long talk with him. He had been in
the prison service for over forty years, most of it spent in Delhi.
He had started off in British times with a salary of Rs 17
per month; in those days he had been able to save ten rupees
every month out of that sum. Now, forty years later at the end
of his career, he was getting just under Rs 400 a month, and
with prices the way they were, he found himself in debt for the
bare necessities of life, not to speak of the expense involved in
the education of his childern and the marriages of his daughters
which were yet to come.

He told us how some years ago about eighty or ninety warders
had been cheated out of seven years pay due to them while on
deputation from the Haryana prison service to Delhi. Neither
the Haryana government nor the Delhi Administration would
pay them, the one passing the buck to the other. In desperation
at the futility of appeals, they had eventually formed a union and
taken the matter to court. After years of litigation the High Court
had finally upheld their claim and ordered that their seven years
wages be paid up. The government responded by quickly transferring all the claimants to different jails, thus effectively scatter-
ing their forces, breaking up the union and sliding out of making

the payment. To date not one of them had been paid for those seven years of work.

"The government rests on its armed forces and its police and jails," the Head Warder said. "If these revolt they will have nothing to protect themselves with. Yet they treat us like dirt. We work day and night, we are short of staff everywhere. Look at me, I am an old man and am not keeping good health, but I am on my feet fourteen hours a day. I literally don't have time to sit down, and yet headquarters won't recruit more men. They say they are short of funds. But look at the waste of money all around you. We see the way money is just thrown down the drain, yet they can't be bothered to look after their own staff. How can they expect loyalty from us?"

It was true. We ourselves had been concerned at the enormous, daily waste of electricity, water, petrol, paper, the travel allowance for police escorts, useless wear and tear on equipment, medicines being thrown away—there was no sense of economy, no concern about wasteful expenditure in the daily routine of jail administration. Take the matter of our own transfer to Hissar from Ambala. The authorities knew very well that all three of us would have to be transferred, yet they sent Kamla in a special van under heavy police guard just ten days before they moved Pushpa and myself the same way. They doubled the cost without a thought, just because of the bureaucratic delay and lack of coordination in passing the orders for our transfer. And this sort of thing was happening with a hundred thousand or more detenus all over the country during the emergency.

In the wards water flowed from the taps all day and night, with no one bothering to turn them off unless it was one of us three. Lights and fans worked all day, even in the cells and barracks which were uninhabited and unused. Prodigal waste accompanied by Scrooge-like tightfistedness abut real needs was the norm. There was not enough fuel with which to cook the prisoners' food, the milk quota for prisoners had been cut because of budgetary restrictions, and they were diddled out of their pay coupons for work done, while the warders were done out of their quota of uniforms and boots, especially in the winter, besides being poorly paid and overworked anyway, all because of the socalled shortage of funds. It was a wonder the warders did not revolt. But they too were held back by fear. They knew that they, like the prisoners, had no right to demand their rights.

When the Central Government's forced sterilization campaign burst upon the country, the state government of Haryana was among the most eager to fulfil and exceed the targets set. Not only was the entire populace, especially the peasants and workers, subjected to the most crude mass sterilizations—irrespective of age, physical fitness or fertility, but government employees, particularly the grade-four employees, were threatened with non-payment of wages, loss of increments and even of their jobs if they did not line up for sterilization in the required time and help fill the required quotas.

The scramble to fill quotas appeared to be synchronised with the visit of the World Bank President, Robert McNamara, to India and it was intriguing to read the press reports of states like Haryana presenting their figures to McNamara even as they handed in their requests for aid and loans from the World Bank. Population control being a favourite McNamara preoccupation, the 'success' of the sterilization campaign seemed to have won his approval of the Indira Gandhi Government with his pronouncement that India had indeed qualified for more aid.

But the people were not so happy. In Hissar, we were told, the police had refused to be sterilized. They informed their superiors that they would be unfit for duty if this was forced on them, and the government quickly backed down. But the jail staff were not so lucky. Although they were extremely reluctant to undergo the operation they were too weak and afraid to refuse and risk their jobs and salaries, so most of them were sterilised.

But this brutal coercion on the part of the government backfired fatally. The reports the warders and matrons gave us of the mayhem outside were confirmed by some of the jail officers and the relatives of prisoners who came on visits to the jail. We were told that the police were stopping buses and trains, hauling people out, herding them into trucks and despatching them to sterilization camps unconcerned whether they were catching old men, unmarried men, men with no children or young boys. Women were spared on the whole because of the more complicated operation involved, but even they had to suffer much indignity and coercion at the hands of the police. Doctors worked round the clock, desperate to fill their set quotas or lose their jobs, turning a blind eye on the rights and wrongs of what they were doing. Villagers were told that irrigation would be cut off from their fields if they did not send sufficient numbers to the camps for sterilization, so the richer farmers, anxious not to lose their crops, herded their farm labour and the village poor into trucks and despatched them to the camps post haste.

However much the sterilization campaign might have impressed McNamara, the people of India, even in remote villages, were brought to the point of revolt against the atrocities committed in its name. Police and medical teams were stoned in the villages and towns, demonstrations and protests grew, and the government's credibility was fast running out. Nobody in jail tried to defend it any longer. In the past the officers had at least tried to avoid politics, and some, especially the more senior ones, tried to defend the government's policies. But now most of them openly voiced their disgust at what was going on. Discontent was rife, and it seemed that the people were at last being roused from their dumb acceptance of the emergency.

As October drew on, the first signs of winter appeared in the air and it was cool in the early mornings and at night. We were unable to sleep outside in the yard behind my cell now, and dragged our cots into the corridor which was fresher than the cells and Pushpa's room. I had regained my serenity after the turmoil of September, but I maintained my 'boycott' of the women because I wanted them to make the first move after they had been able to understand why I had withdrawn from them.

Nirmala was the first to take the initiative. She confronted me in my cell one afternoon and demanded that I talk to her. I called her in and asked what she wanted.

"I just want you to talk to me," she burst out. "I can't stand your silence any longer. *Didi* I feel terrible; I know how badly I have behaved, I know how upset you have been and how much pain all of us have caused you. You even fell ill because of it— we all know it was because of that. But please give me a chance. I am trying to stop carrying tales to the warders and officers about the others, I have seen for myself how harmful it is. But I just can't control my temper as yet. It blinds me and I just get carried away. My other weakness is that I get swayed by anything I am told—I believe all the rot they pour into my ears and don't wait to find out if it's true or false. I am a fool, a thick-headed Jat, you know this! But I am trying, so don't refuse to talk to me any more, I can't bear it."

I told her that I had only stopped talking to the women because they had chosen to go their own way of tearing each other (and us as well) apart with the venom of their quarrels. Our way, my way, was the way of the *panchayat*, but they had rejected that. Until they saw this was the only way to solve their problems, I did not think it was any use talking further to them.

"*Didi*," she said, "we have tried your way, and we have seen it work in practice in Ambala. We all know that it is the only way for us, but we are too stupid and headstrong to maintain it, and we are hurting only ourselves as a result. Everyone says this. Already the officers are saying that we are a bad lot anyway. Well, this is my resolution, I can only speak for myself just now. Until I change myself I cannot try to change the others. Just give me a couple of weeks—see, ever since I realised how harmful it was to carry tales against the others I have stopped doing that," she grinned. "It was quite an effort I'm telling you!" and we both laughed. "Now what remains is my terrible temper. I see red without rhyme or reason and quarrel over nothing, but give me time to control this too and then I'll tackle the others."

"Why Nirmala," I said hugging her, "you are such a sensible girl when you're sane. This is excellent. Go ahead and do your best. As long as you are honestly trying, you know that you can always count on me to help you."

She went away and was as good as gold for several weeks after this. The other women, seeing that Nirmala and I were friends again, tried to resume normal relations as well. But I made it clear that this was not a question of 'kiss and make up'; they must realise what had happened and be prepared to admit where they had gone wrong.

October 22 was the festival of Divali, the festival of lights, of the triumph of good over evil when Lord Rama slew the demon god Ravana. That evening Pushpa and I were playing badminton as usual when the '*goonda* party' as we had christened the most truculent of the women, Dhanni, Maya and Nirmala, and two or three others, came up to us somewhat hesitantly.

We took no notice and went on with our game. After a while they came on to Pushpa's court and asked how long we would be.

"A little longer, we're almost done," Pushpa told them.

"But then they'll lock us up," said Maya, "we'll stop you now!"

They gathered up the net and then they advanced towards me.

"Are you going to beat me up?" I asked.

They surrounded me and then, putting their arms around me, they stuffed my mouth with the sweets they had brought. Nirmala pranced around us, jumping up and down and shouting, "I'm so happy, I'm so happy. At last they've done it! Every day Maya and Dhanni have been saying how much they are longing to speak to *Didi*, but are too scared of her—and now at last they've done it. I kept telling them to go ahead, *Didi* is not illiterate like us, she won't snub you, is what I told them. And now at last it's done!"

It was not the time to lecture them about what still remained unsaid. I wanted them to realise that it was not a question of 'burying the past' and letting bygones be. Somehow they must see what had happened as a guide to the future. But now the spirit of Divali had gripped us all and warmth and goodwill flowed.

Some days later Dhanni came to me.

"*Didi*," she said, "I want you to know something. You get so upset when we fight, but you should realise that we ourselves don't take it so seriously. You can't stop us fighting—it's in our blood. We will fight one day and be friends the next. We have learned the value of the lessons you have tried to teach us. We know how important unity is, and we will unite when the need arises. But till then we will continue to fight and squabble amongst ourselves and you must just ignore us."

She was right in a way, I suppose. In any case the more serious aspects of "their way" versus mine would take time to mature. Until then I would take Dhanni's advice.

The year was drawing to an end. In December, Charles and Karoki were coming out to India for Christmas with my family. I would be able to see Charles only twice as he was to be in the country for only two weeks. Karoki I would see four times, and then he would go back to England.

The first meeting was with Karoki, my mother and my sister, Charles having left him with them in Delhi where my sister now lived, and gone on to the Far East on a business trip. Karoki was wearing his English school uniform, and with his English accent and strange formality I felt a bit uneasy with him at first. Then he came to me, sat in my lap, pressed his cheek against mine and was the Karoki I had always known. He told me about his school in England. He liked it, but was finding it hard to make friends. He said it was easier to make friends in India than in England. Realising that this was a rather special interview the jail authorities allowed us a little over the hour normally given. When it was over and time to leave, Karoki whispered in my ear, "Try your best and come home for Christmas."

Each Thursday for four weeks I saw him. The last visit was with Charles and Karoki on 6 January 1977. After this Charles was to fly back to England via Cairo on the 8th, and Karoki was to follow direct on the 12th. I had been dreading this last visit. All week I had felt too wretched to be able to contemplate another indefinite parting from Karoki with equanimity. Without saying a word he had been able to communicate, just by the way he sat close in my arms, pressing his head and cheek to mine, all that he felt and wanted. He did not cry or complain and indeed was remarkably composed and calm, but I knew what a battle he had waged. Starting a totally new life in England with his father away at work, no friends, and an empty house to come back to had not been easy. He had won through, I could see that, and was deeply grateful for it. In fact it was Charles and my parents and sister above all who had given him the love and the support, the strength and understanding which had helped him to be as stable and strong as he was. But the loneliness and friendlessness of life in England was what I dreaded for him. He would have to go back soon, and the warmth and vitality of India would no longer be available to him.

January 6 came, and I was called out for the interview. I had managed to gain full control over myself after a lot of thought in the last day or two and the farewells went off smoothly. Karoki seemed to have decided his line of struggle too. He kept a certain distance from me this time and spent most of the visit sending

paper darts skimming across the room with the jail officers and
CID men ducking good humouredly out of the way. Smiling and
calm as always, Karoki made sure not to come too close to me
that day. He was looking a bit pale and strained, and I could see
how hard it was for him and what strength the little boy posses-
sed already. So we were able to make it easy for each other and
I was grateful to Karoki for his help.

On Saturday 9 January 1977 I was having my bath in the morning when the matron called out to say that the "Dipty Sahib"
was waiting outside my cell to see me. I dressed quickly and went
out. He was smiling.

"Congratulations Mrs Lewis, here is a telegram for you."

I took it from him. It read: "Release on parole ordered. Will
collect you twelve noon en route Chandigarh. Charles Karoki."

Suddenly, out of the blue, the Gods had decided to release
me. My first reaction was one of sharp anger. How dare they, I
thought. First they imprison one for no good reason and nothing
one can say or do will make them relent and then they let one
go—flip, with a snap of the fingers. The bastards! I thought of
Pushpa being left here, and my first reaction to the news was
hardly happy. The problem of the prisoners too remained unre-
solved. I had envisaged the slow unravelling of it over a long incarceration—now I may not have the opportunity for that. Had
anything of what we had tried to communicate to them taken
root, or would the turbulent waves of frustration and fear engulf
them completely once again? Arbitrarily thrown together, arbitrarily separated, the life and the intensity of experience shared
with them seemed a gift not fully granted before it was taken
away. Then the thought of the dear faces I would see again began
to stir something deep inside me and excitement began to well up.

Pushpa came running to my cell, full of joy at the news and
brave about the prospect of being left behind. The women
gathered round and some of them began to cry, until Maya
turned on them: "Let her go. It's high time she went back to her
family. Let us pray that *Barri Didi* too will go home soon. You
have done all you could for us and though we feel as if our only
support is leaving, we wish you all the joy of going back to your
people again."

We waited together in Pushpa's room after I had packed my things, and distributed as much as I could amongst the women. Then I was called into the office where I found Charles, Karoki and my mother waiting for me. Karoki said "Hi!" with a big grin. I was shown the order and conditions for my release on parole. I was to be released for three months if I agreed to remain within the limits of the Union Territory of Chandigarh, avoid all direct and indirect political activity, give no statement or interviews to the press, and surrender myself into the custody of the Superintendent, Hissar Borstal Jail on 9 April 1977.

I signed the conditions and was given the cash and personal effects that had been kept by the jail authorities all this while. My mother distributed sweets and the jail officers came to say goodbye. They insisted that this was goodbye, as once parole was granted it was rare for any one to come back. I slipped back into the ward for a minute to say a last farewell and to tell everyone that I would be seeing them again in three months time.

"God forbid!" was the chorus.

Pushpa and I embraced without a word and she watched me go out with a bright smile.

On the way to Chandigarh I heard the story of my release. Charles had spent practically every moment of his time in India trying to secure my release but with no success. He was told that although the Home Ministry had passed orders for my release twice, signed by the Home Minister himself, the Delhi Administration, which was virtually being run by Navin Chawla in the name of the Lt. Governor, had blocked these each time and there was nothing the Home Ministry could do about it because of Chawla's special relationship with Sanjay Gandhi. Charles was to have left on 8 January, and it was only on the night of the 7th that he was informed that I would be released on parole. But the written order had to be procured from the Lt. Governor, and it had taken a whole suspense-filled day before it came through late in the evening of the 8th, just before all government offices closed for the weekend. To the last it was anyone's guess whether the papers would be blocked yet again.

So Charles postponed his departure by four days and sent a cable to Karoki's Headmaster requesting another three weeks leave for him. We would never know what made the Delhi Administration change its mind and let me go. Perhaps it was the

letter Karoki had written to Mrs Gandhi some weeks before, one
night in Oxford, when he had been feeling especially sad. He had
drawn a large picture of me behind bars with an inscription
saying "LET ME OUT OF HERE!" And the letter read:

"Dear Mrs Gandhi,

Could you please let Mrs Primila Lewis out, because I am
missing her a lot and I haven't seen her for a long time.

Karoki Lewis."

Whatever it was, we were thankful to be together again, even
if it was only for a short while.

4

"The global redistribution of power leads us step by step, choice by choice, to a socialist society, nothing less. As a guide in making these choices, we might refer to the following principles:

'... men before machines, people before governments, practice before theory, student before teacher, countryside before city, smallness before bigness, wholeness before reductionism, organic before synthetic, plants before animals, craftsmanship before expertise, quality before quantity...' and, I would add, questions before answers.

To my mind, development is about making such choices, at home and overseas. It is about challenging those who reject these priorities. It is about taking sides; and in this game, nobody is a spectator."

Glyn Roberts, in *Questioning Development*.

IT WAS WONDERFUL TO BE ABLE TO TALK TO MY FAMILY without the intelligence men and jailors breathing down our necks. My father and sister drove up from Delhi on the evening of my release. My father said little as usual, but an immense burden seemed to have slipped off his shoulders, and he listened quietly while the rest of us chattered on late into the night catching up with all that we had not been able to talk about at the interviews in prison. That very evening I had a telephone call from Kamla from her home in Yamunanagar. She had been released unconditionally on the 7th, and had received a wire from my sister on the 8th, informing her of my parole. After a bare week with her family, she was to be swept into an exhausting election campaign although her health had by no means recovered.

We met in Chandigarh about two weeks later when she came to spend a night with me. Troubled by the knowledge that she would probably not be allowed the opportunity to develop her work and ideas along the lines we had so often discussed in jail, she prepared herself to accept the consequences of an election which might at least result in bringing an end to nineteen months of fascism under the emergency.

Pushpa was still in prison. The government had included her name on a list of those detenus who were to be released immediately, but there were harassing delays and it took almost a month before she too was released unconditionally.

On 17 January Mrs Gandhi announced a general election to

be held in March. Slowly the people who had been cramped by nineteen months of terror awakened to life again. Four major opposition parties, the Socialist Party, the Bharatya Lok Dal, the Old Congress and the Jan Sangh, hurriedly united to form the Janata Party with the blessings of Jayaprakash Narayan. The Communist Party of India (Marxist) and various regional parties like the Akali Dal in the Punjab and the Dravida Munnetra Kazgham in Tamil Nadu, extended full support to the Janata Party. Only a united opposition stood any chance against Mrs Gandhi, and although most of the opposition party members had been released they were given precious little time to organise themselves before the elections sixty days ahead.

The disarray of the opposition, and the fear and suspicion in the people that this call for elections might be just another gimmick or even a trap, resulted in a sluggish start to the campaign. But the sudden defection of Jagjivan Ram, a cabinet minister and leading Congressman who left the ruling party along with some others to form the Congress for Democracy, extending full support to the Janata Party, changed the atmosphere dramatically. For the first time the cracks and fissures in the Congress Party led by Mrs Gandhi were exposed for all to see. Taking heart from this the people were emboldened to express at last their resentment and anger against the emergency and the atrocities committed in its name.

Excitement mounted. The government tried every way, by fair means and foul, to prevent the enthusiastic crowds from attending opposition rallies and meetings. They stopped public transport, switched off power for loud-speakers at meetings, put up barricades and stopped public transport, threatened the people with more emergency, bribed them with tax-free cinema hits and put on special television shows, but nothing could stem the tide of people pouring into the places where opposition leaders were holding rallies and making speeches.

The Janata Party, with its election manifesto promising an end to dictatorship and the black deeds of the fascist Indira Gandhi regime, was carried to an overwhelming victory when all the results were declared by March 20th. Mrs Gandhi, her son Sanjay, and every one of her caucus of stooges including the Defence Minister Bansilal, the Minister for Information and Broadcasting V.C. Shukla and the Law Minister Gokhale were routed at the polls. Along with the Congress defeat its chief ally, the Communist Party of India, was also decimated. Mrs Gandhi's last act as Prime Minister was to revoke the emergency. It was a magnificent victory for the people. But the problems facing them were of a sobering magnitude.

I think of what that great fighter for India's freedom, Lala Lajpat Rai, wrote in 1915, in a pamphlet called *Reflections on the Potitical Situation in India:*

> The prosperity of a country must be judged by the economic position of the wage earner, and judged from that point of view it can be conclusively proved that the wage-earning classes are in effect much poorer today than they were ever before. That is the explanation of the increase in lawlessness all over the country.

And in an *Open Letter to Lloyd George* in 1917, he wrote:

> At present they (the Indian people) are let to exist but not to live. More than a 100 million are insufficiently fed. At least 60 million do not get two meals a day. . . . They work and toil and sweat primarily in the interests of the British capitalist and secondarily in the interests of his Indian colleague. The latter only gets the leavings of the former. . . . The profits of agriculture are divided between your government and the big landlords. The pressure on land has reduced the ryot's holdings, while the number of mouths requiring food and the number of bodies requiring clothing has increased.
>
> Your government encourages drinking, speculating and gambling in a way never before conceived.

Set this against what an important Congressman is reported to have said in 1977: "When the Congress Party announced its programme of Socialism in 1955, thirty-four per cent of the population was below the poverty line. Mrs Gandhi's *Garibi Hatao* programme brought that figure up to seventy per cent by 1975."

The 20-Point Programme of the emergency may have raised it even beyond that.

Although there are some good people in the new government, all the basic problems remain. Even though the restoration of

democracy, the release of all political prisoners and the revoca-
tion of all detention laws were a main plank of the election manifesto that swept it to victory, the Janata Government has not been
able to redeem any of these promises in full. The Prime Minister,
Mr Morarji Desai, had claimed that a Janata government would
make it impossible for an emergency ever to be imposed on the
people again. But the hard fact is that as long as the fundamental
economic and social problems remain, and the authoritarianism
of a small elite over the masses of the people stays intact, the
crisis of India will continue to deepen and we can expect one
emergency to follow another.

Thus, if Mrs Gandhi's emergency is over Mr Desai's perhaps
has just begun. The beautiful slogans of the election manifesto
and the new economic programme of the government seem destin-
ed to remain on paper in the same way as the *Garibi Hatao* and
20-Point Programmes of Mrs Gandhi. But if revolution is the
only answer to India's problems, the revolutionary left seems to
have a long way to go before it can become an effective force. In
fact the spontaneous struggles of the people have outstripped
the Left in general, and the 'vanguard' role of the latter is rarely
to be seen. All appears dark and moribund. But the new young
shoots of life are hidden deep among the people, and these will
blossom and bear fruit one day.

Both my jail comrades are ministers in their respective state
assemblies. I wonder if they ever think about our conversations
in jail, and how we had agreed that only when the masses of our
people became conscious of the real meaning of democracy and
the fact that they must fight for it, would our country be free
and strong. That our task was to go among the people in order
to educate and organise them to this end—not to bribe and
bamboozle them for votes every five years so that we could then
sit tight and devour the fruits of electoral victories ourselves.
Today, surrounded as my jail mates must be with sychophants
and lackeys, most of whom have simply jumped off the old band-
wagon and on to the new, I wonder what they think.

As for me, when the emergency was revoked, I was finally free
and went to Delhi where I met Srilata and my friends again. Sri
and I went to Mehrauli, and the workers who gathered to meet
us told of all that had passed in the intervening months. They had
suffered daily harassment from the CID and many had been

thrown out of their jobs. The revised Minimum Wages had nowhere been paid, although most farm workers were getting a better deal now than they had in the past. Throughout the emergency and despite the watch on them, some of them had managed to continue to hold meetings, and they had tried to keep the union alive.

"We want you to come back to us," they said, "but we know that this is difficult for you now. Even if you can't come back to us, we know the way forward. It will be slower and more difficult without you, but we will make it. We have to. There is no other way."

On 28 June 1977 I caught the British Airways flight to Heathrow. It was Karoki's 10th birthday and I had promised to be with him by then. But India calls, and I will go back. I have to, because my place is there.

December, 1977

Appendix

(This is the statement I had written from jail, to be read in the High Court along with my Writ Petition.)

I would like to state at the outset that I am not a lawyer and I do not claim to understand legal technicalities. I am, however, a mature and thinking citizen of my country. I happen to belong to that small number of people in the middle class who are privileged to have received the best that relative wealth, formal education and a liberal upbringing can give.

Living in the USA and England taught me, for the first time, what democracy and democratic consciousness mean. The people of these countries have struggled for their democracy for centuries and are alert to it today. Living in Africa, I came to understand the ravages of colonialism, ironically perpetrated by these very democracies. One of the greatest damages done, as I saw it, was the reduction of the middle class intelligentsia to a state of mimicking, pseudo-westernized impotency. And this handful of tailors' dummies were the ruling elite. I recognised myself as one of them and returned to India determined to give up teaching English Literature and to learn instead about my country, its people, their poverty and backwardness and what I could do, as a responsible and awakened citizen, to help in the process of change.

But I soon saw, when I returned, that I could not do this in an abstract or haphazard way. I could only learn about the people by going to them, and I could only go to them if I had something concrete and useful to offer them.

So began a new education, my first real education.

In the tenements and shacks of Bombay's slums, where we had started some supplementary nights schools for children and library facilities for adults, I made friends with people who were living, whole families of them, in a space something like five feet by two feet. I learned that the men, who worked in factories, spent their wages on films, transistor radios, terylene shirts and terycot trousers, while their wives had nothing but a single torn sari and no food to cook at home. I watched their children playing on garbage heaps and scrabbling for pickings in the filth. In the monsoon the whole area became a river of excrement, garbage and muddy water, waist high, flooding the roads, houses, everything. I saw the rotten vegetables, worm-eaten, stale and decomposed, which the people bought for their daily food.

These people—living uncomplainingly in conditions of total degradation and squalor, squandering their earnings on drink, on *matka* gambling, on the incessantly advertised thrills of the cinema, film songs, terycot—were hardened, cynical and wary of all do-gooders, sociologists, journalists, politicians. They had seen plenty of them, and they had learned one hard lesson from them: these people only come to us for what they can get out of us.

Disconcerting, but true. These people had seen everything. They saw right through us too, and they rejected us. And they were right. Who were we to descend on them and patronize them with our good intentions? I saw the real failure of most social work organisations: they turn people into shameless beggars and cynical opportunists. The point is to waken them into a consciousness of their condition and the need to change it by their own unified effort. This was the real meaning of the struggle for democracy.

When my husband was transferred to Delhi at the end of 1971, we decided to live on a farm in Mehrauli rather than in one of the crowded colonies of the city, to send our child to the local village school and to simplify our own life style as far as we could. I also decided to get to know our neighbours. These were the immigrant *purabias* working on the farms and the simple village folk living all around us.

As I got to know them and their families, I began to learn

about their problems and share their troubles with them as well. We became friends in a simple and genuine way, and it was borne on me that these people, and millions of others like them, were the real people of India. So far 'poverty' and 'the poor' had been more or less of an intellectual abstraction to me. Now these people brought home the fact that 'democracy', 'progress', 'human rights', the 'dignity of man', were not just for well-fed upper-class intellectuals like myself, but for every man, woman and child in this country. These people had the same, the very same, inalienable, 'fundamental rights' as any one of my kind. They *had* to have, they *must* have, these basic human rights. Otherwise there would be no hope for us at all. No hope for progress, change, development. No hope for India.

Quite simply, my friendship with these people broke down the barriers that we, the upper classes, have so long and so successfully built between ourselves and the poor. It is the brilliantly simple technique of switching our minds off, just not seeing them as the same species as ourselves, so that democracy, freedom, 'rights', are all for us alone. These people are simply not human. We have conveniently dehumanised them, and only regard their encroachment on our consciousness as, at best, a tedious nuisance, and at worst, a problem to be solved by others—usually the police!

To most of us, it is a matter of course, quite normal, natural, that millions of people should have no homes, no clothes on their backs, no food in their stomachs, and no voice for their pain. Foreigners coming to the cities of India are appalled, revolted, oppressed by the degradation of human life all around them. But we step over the open sores and stinking corpses, noses held high, eyes only on the next round of entertainment or consumption of the good things of life, gorging and stuffing ourselves, avoiding the ravenous hunger in the glazed eyes of the tattered rabble pressing around us.

Well, I couldn't do that any longer; each mouthful I swallowed sounded the same alarm: till the next man can eat, what right have you to do so? And the 'next man' was no longer an abstraction. He was Ram Pher and Budh Ram, Mata Prasad and Rameshwar, Budhan and Laloo—who had the same needs as I did, who had the same flesh and blood and brains as any one of us, but who had been ground down into a worm-like existence through sheer deprivation of his fundamental, inalienable human rights. And his children, brimming with intelligence and life, would be ground down, ground out in the same way.

It was a painful realisation, indeed, that three-fourths of our people have been denied the means to realise themselves as human beings, with the full rights, responsibilities and dignity of free citizens in a free country. Till they had these means, there could be no hope for this country, and these means could only come about through their own realisation of the need for them: their own awareness, their own struggle. Such things as democratic rights and responsibilities cannot be gifted, bestowed or imposed. They must be realised consciously through a continuous process of conscious endeavour. I had to help them to become aware.

All these ideas are well enshrined in the Constitution of India and in the writings and speeches of all our leaders. Indeed, I started out inspired by the *Garibi Hatao* programme of 1971—and even today the needs of the poor are on every political lip, as well as being a pivot of the 20-Point Programme. I am aware that there is nothing original in my thinking. I only wish to state that my thinking, my understanding of these well-worn ideals, impelled me to translate them into action, to implement them practically, and not rest content with having theorised about them.

Take the problem of medical aid. When Kaloo Ram's wife was seriously ill, it seemed normal that the local government clinic or the Safdarjung Hospital were the obvious places for her treatment. Kaloo Ram's extreme reluctance to go to either must be overcome. He would rather fork out what were for him huge sums of money to a private quack in Mehrauli, than get free medical attention from the qualified government doctors in these hospitals. I soon understood why. The poor have no voice in the hospitals ostensibly set up for them. If you are poor, illiterate and ignorant, you are treated with contempt and dislike. There is no time for you, no medicine for you, no bed for you, no room for you. You are shunted from pillar to post, told to come back another day, told to go buy medicines from the chemist outside, told anything to get rid of you. You, who earn four rupees a day, have given up your day's wages to come this far by bus. No, Kaloo Ram, and countless others like him, would rather die than go to a government hospital.

But I have noticed that people like myself never have any trouble in these hospitals. We, who can afford private medication, dominate the doctor's time and attention to the exclusion of the desperately needy who are simply ignored.

I used to go with the sick myself, and this way they were attended to promptly and carefully. But is this the way it should be? And how is this situation to be changed if it is wrong? I tried to educate the people about the workings of the hospital, the signs they could not read, where to go for which problem, how to talk to the *chaprasis*, nurses and doctors simply and clearly, without fear—and gradually how to have the confidence to say to themselves: I *will* go to a government hospital, it has been built for me, it is my right to be treated like a citizen and not like a dog in the streets.

The same story was repeated in every department that related in some way to the lives of the Mehrauli poor. The Post Office, the Block Development Office, the *Tehsil*, the Veterinary Clinic, the Family Planning Clinic. To be a citizen and not a dog or a slave or a serf, is a two-way process. I must get my rights certainly but I must deserve them too. It was this two-way process, this struggle for dignity and the right to dignity, responsible citizenship and the rights of citizenship that I saw as the fundamental need.

But it soon became apparent that dignity was a far cry for people who had to struggle like wild beasts just to be able to eat. Without any kind of security even as to where the next meal was to come from, those *purabia* labourers were not likely to worry overmuch about their dignity. You can be poor with dignity, but you cannot be degraded with dignity. These people were degraded. Degraded by the sheer circumstance of their lives: degraded by history, by society, by economy, administration and by *rule*.

Harijans first, illiterate, landless labourers, deep in debt for generations, immigrants in the city, certified as 'homeless', rooting about in the mines, quarries, brick kilns and farms of Delhi for 'unskilled' work. Ready to snap up any crumb thrown their way, fight among themselves for it, and jump like a shot into a fellow-*purabia's* job for just five rupees less. Frightened of everybody: the money-lender and *thakur* back home, the *malik*, the police, the officer, all *sahibs* of the city, and above all, terrified of the hostile *Jat* and *Gujar* residents of the villages. We are *Pardesis*—we have no rights here and can claim none. We are here on sufferance. If the villagers don't like us, if we offend them in any way, they will drive us out.

Free citizens in a free country? It is an age of terrible darkness, terrible hypocrisy, if we claim this. Right under the nose of the Capital is a starkly medieval situation for thousands upon thousands of immigrant workers—and these are a fraction of the numbers in total all over our country.

Moreover, as I came to learn, these people, when and where they did find work, especially under contract in the mines, quarries and brick works, were no better than bonded labourers. Held in bondage by 'advances' loaned at the outset of a contract, their lives, the honour of their wives, the labour of their children, all were at the mercy of the contractor. The account of the 'advances' is kept in his own inimitable fashion by the contractor, who adds interest and other entries over the year, and presents them with a bill at the end of it, of sometimes as much as two or three thousand rupees, when the original 'advance' was no more than a hundred rupees. So the labourer is trapped for years in the clutches of a contractor who will continue to pay out 'advances' for him to keep body and soul together, while he and his family wear themselves out to pay back a debt which never diminishes.

The contractor numbs the workers with cheap liquor at night, makes free with their wives and sisters at his pleasure and, if anyone dares to resist, thinks nothing of beating them or burning down their jhuggies and, as in the notorious case in Mandi/Jaunapur villages early in 1975, letting a few children roast alive in the flames as well.

No mining laws were evident anywhere in the Mehrauli *tehsil*, and no labour laws either. The farm workers, employed by some of the most illustrious names of our country (pillars of government, industry the administration and the armed forces, not to speak of one-time *rajas* and *maharajas*), were hired at nominal wages of eighty or ninety rupees a month, made to work all day, responsible as *chowkidars* at night, no time off, fired at will—on farms, most of them highly intensive and mechanised, which were sending roses to Europe, grapes and peaches to the tables of the rich, and wheat and rice to the black markets of the city. These farms themselves are a gold mine in real-estate investment, hidden wealth, black money turned to white, not to speak of smuggled treasures discovered on their premises.

I paid a visit to the Labour Ministry, where, on saying at the reception that I wanted to find out something about Labour laws and other legislation regarding the problems of labour in the Mehrauli area, I was directed to the Library. But on my saying that I was ignorant of even the rudiments of law and wouldn't know where to look, a gentleman very kindly informed me about various labour laws in operation and told me that I must get the workers registered as a Union under the Trade Union Act—unless they were unionised no amount of legislation could make any difference to them. It simply would not be implemented.

It was a sobering task, as I had no experience of Trade Union work, and also because the people I knew best were the farm workers who were generally not more than two or three, and quite often only one, on a farm, and widely scattered over a large area. But it was obvious that only some form of organised activity would help them. And so we—those few whom I knew best and who were eager to work for new ideas, and I—began the long, slow and extremely difficult job of going from farm to farm, organising meetings in small groups and explaining the meaning of and the need for a Union. I want to emphasise that our concept of a Union was rather different to the traditional concept of trade unionism as it has come to be accepted. Our effort was to eliminate, step by step, all the obstacles, both internal and external, to our lives as decent human beings and enlightened citizens, through sincere collective effort and struggle. We must remove our own tendencies towards mutual mistrust, strife, dishonesty, laziness, fear, casteism, communalism, provincialism. We must genuinely unite and try to solve all our own problems collectively. Only when we were on firm ground ourselves, when we knew that we were putting in solid, honest work ourselves, could we stand fearlessly for the demand: fair wages for fair work. We would ask for eight hours pay for eight hours work. We would not be content with four hours pay for eight hours work, nor would we demand eight hours pay for four hours work. Our problems were serious enough and there was no need to falsify or exaggerate our claim. But once we knew that a claim was fair, we would struggle on doggedly until it was met. Our procedure, as we worked it out, was to ascertain all claims locally first, then approach the employer in writing, informing him of the claim of his employee and requesting his views in reply, and only after hearing all sides of the case would we press our claim.

Sometimes false claims were registered with us. As soon as these were discovered, the workers unanimously—through their Executive Committee, and after thorough discussion in their area meetings—rejected them as betraying the interests of the Union, which was struggling for justice and was not an opportunistic bargain counter.

We also decided against joining any political party or organisation. There was no such party in the area, and we wanted to concentrate on our own problems. If any party wanted to help us, or any individual wanted to work with us, we would welcome them as long as they worked in the interests of the Mehrauli workers and according to the principles of our Union, and not for their own political ends at the expense of these interests. Thus, although once our Union was established in the area we attracted the notice of various political parties such as the Congress, the Socialist Party, the Communist Party of India, (Marxist) and the Communist Party of India (CPI), we have maintained our independence from all of them. But recently—only in May 75—our workers took the decision to affiliate with the All-India Trade Union Congress, as in practice we had found the CPI the most consistent and sincere in its help and support of our work. However, to date, neither I nor, as far as I am aware, any member of the Dehat Mazdoor Union (DMU) has joined any political party or organisation.

Our intention was not to force confrontation and agitation, but to develop a recognition and understanding of our basic human rights as citizens of this society. We expected a sympathetic response from all those who proclaim so vociferously the urgent need for precisely this kind of consciousness in our downtrodden masses, if democracy is to be realised in practice. Our dismay at the totally opposite reaction we got instead from the VIP farm owners, when finally, after over a year and a half of patient organising work, we registered the Dehat Mazdoor Union in February 1973, can be imagined.

The initial reaction of the employers was to simply ignore us. Despite our slender resources (the Union fee was Re 1/ for membership, Rs 4/ as annual subscription), we sent all letters by registered post, each such letter eating into more than a third of the annual subscription of each worker. Expenses on postage alone left us with almost nothing to take cases forward to the law courts etc.,—where transportation alone could add up to more than a man earned in a day.

But, when the immediate reaction of the employer is one of total hostility, and he calls in the police to evict his worker who has dared to mention a *claim* under the *law* before him—and when, on the police being informed that they have no right to evict persons involved in a dispute with their employer without a court order, their response is—'There is no such law, there is no such thing as a labour court for you people, you are being misled by this Mrs Lewis, just do what your *malik* tells you or you will be in trouble' (this from the SHO Mehrauli)—and when to make these threats real, the police rig up case after case of theft, trespass, riot, assault on innocent workers, involving them in the tragically expensive, wasteful procedures of the criminal courts—and when complaints of harassment, threats, assault on the workers by the employers and their friends are not even registered by the police—and when committee members are beaten up by the hirelings of these employers in their own office premises and then arrested for assault and trespass themselves. . . when these things happen in a cumulative chain reaction to the simple, entirely lawful claim for basic legal rights, you can imagine the cost involved—financial, as well as in terms of faith in the sanctity of the laws of this land.

Time and time again we made representations to the higher authorities—the SP South, the SDM and ADM South, the IG Police, the DC, Delhi, the Executive Councellor, O.P. Behl, the Labour Commissioner, and time and again we got the same reply—verbally of course, never in writing. We sympathise with your work, your aims are noble, your demands are entirely reasonable—but you have chosen the wrong area. The farm owners are all VIPs. They are too powerful for us to handle. We dare not command *them* to obey the laws. You will have to rely on your own strength, but we advise you to pick another area for your work—you will be in trouble if you don't.

We are too poor to go to the civil courts for redress of wrongs done by the police on behalf of their VIP employers. We are too poor to be able to wait, month after month for our wages while the Labour Court goes through the motions of negotiations and conciliation. We are too poor to stand bail for thousands of rupees for each wretched *purabia* hauled up on a trumped-up case in the Criminal Courts. We are too poor to allow the single breadwinner in the family to rot in jail without bail while his wife and children starve to death at home. We are too poor to afford letter after letter sent by Registered Acknowledgement Due post to employers who tear them up on seeing they are from the Union. We are too poor to by bus tickets from the villages of Mehrauli to the courts at Parliament Street, Rajpur Road, and the New Courts. If the Labour Laws that have been passed in our interests are not meant to be implemented, if the Minimum Wages Act, the Factories Act, the Industrial Disputes Act, the Contract Labourers Act, the Shops and Establishments Act, the Mining Laws, the Workers' Compensation Act, are just pieces of paper—we shall not be able to afford the legal processes and procedures that we have killed ourselves trying to follow in order to win our rights.

If the naked violation of every law of the land is possible for the VIP owners of the farms in Mehrauli, if the police are to nakedly help in the violation of these laws, if the administration in our capital city is helpless to contain these flagrant violations of even our minimum legal rights, then what price democracy and the rule of law?

I challenge anybody in the police or administration, who has the courage to be honest, to state that we in the Dehat Mazdoor Union have ever knowingly or wilfully adopted any illegal steps or practices. Yes, we have held demonstrations of protest, we have shouted slogans, we have held gate meetings, we have struck work—but not a single one of these activities was illegal at the time, i.e., before the emergency. And when it is remembered that each meeting, each demonstration means a day's wages lost let it be clear that these were resorted to only in extremity, when every other means of persuasion had failed.

That news of our struggle for the implementation of minimum legal rights by wealthy and powerful employers who were flouting every possible law including the very registration of their farms, factories and mines in the area as profit making enterprises, reached the Press is not surprising. It is not surprising that questions were raised in both houses of Parliament regarding this appalling state of affairs. It is not surprising that minimum wages have become a clarion cry all over the country during the emergency. That some of us had to go to jail under the Maintenance of Internal Security Act and the Defence of India Rules for having struggled legally for the legal rights which every government minister and politician is proclaiming from every rooftop, and that the people flouting the law and utilising their power and position to protect themselves have tried to crush that legitimate struggle by the oppressed, downtrodden, unorganised section of our people for their minimum legal rights and the chance to become human beings instead of trodden worms is painful, serious and sobering, if not surprising.

In conclusion I would like to say that both individually and in my capacity as a founder worker in the Dehat Mazdoor Union, I have always believed in democracy and the rule of law, and I have always protested against injustice, illegality and brutality. I believe that I have been wrongfully confined—but if democracy and the rule of law themselves are being confined, then I accept my confinement cheerfully, and am confident that justice, legality and human rights will ultimately and victoriously prevail.

Glossary

Angithi	brazier
Ashram	religious retreat
Ashtmi	8th day of the lunar calendar
Aspatal	hospital
Atta	wheat flour
Awara-gardi	loitering, vagrancy
Ayurvedic	system of Indian medicine dating from Vedic times, or traditional Hindu science of medicine
Babus	urban educated people
Bajra	kind of millet
Bania	trader, money-lender
Banyani	wife of a *bania*
Bhaiya	brother, term used in Eastern Uttar Pradesh and Bihar for the 'lower orders'
Bhang	marijuana
Bhangi	sweeperess, untouchable
Behnchod	sister-fucker
Behnji	sister
Bidi	cheap tobacco rolled in leaf
Chaddar	sheet or veil
Chakkar	circle, syndrome
Chamar	leather worker, untouchable
Chamcha	stooge, lackey
Chapati	unleavened bread
Chaprasis	orderlies, office messengers

Chara	fodder
Charkha	spinning wheel
Charpai	light string bedstead or cot
Chowk	square, crossing
Chowkidar	watchman
Chudi	sweeperess, untouchable
Chuggli	carrying tales
Dada	bullyboy, gang leader
Dal	lentils
Daphter-walli	the woman in the office
Daura	a kind of fit
Deharidar	daily wage worker
Dehat	rural area
Dehati	rural dweller and his language
Devi	Goddess
Dharna	sit in, picket
Dhobi	washerman
Dholak	small drum
Didi	elder sister
Dipty Sahib	deputy sahib
Durbar	royal court
Durree	cotton rug
Garibi Hatao	remove, abolish poverty
Ghara	earthen pitcher
Goonda	hired rowdy, thug
Gujar	cattle-owning tribe or community
Hissab	dues, account
Izzat	honour, self-respect
Jamadar	labour contractor and headman
Jat	peasant farmers, a sub-caste
Jhuggi	slum dwelling, mud hut
Kali Mem	black lady
Karma	actions, destiny
Kirtan	devotional songs
Kheer	rice pudding
Khota	bad, false
Khurpi	trowel
Lal Topi	red cap
Langar	community kitchen
Lathi	iron-tipped stave or stick

Lungi	sarong
Mahatma	great soul
Mai-baap	dependence on paternalism; likrally, mother-father
Mali	gardener, farm worker
Malik	owner, employer
Manji	string bed, cot
Mast	oblivious
Mataji	mother, used as a term of respect
Matka	illegal betting, gambling in state of Maharashtra
Mussalman	Muslim
Namaste	greeting
Nav ratri	nine nights, a ten-day period of worship of the goddess Durga
Numberdarni	female convict in charge of ward under matrons and warders
Paishi	to be produced before the authorities; here, the Jail Superintendent
Panchayat	village council
Panchayat ghar	council house
Pardesi	alien, foreigner
Pradhan	head of village council
Purabia	easterner, specifically used for one from the states of Uttar Pradesh and Bihar
Rajas and *Maharajas*	princely rulers
Rajmata	dowager queen
Rakshasa	demon
Ramayana	Hindu religious epic
Rand	widow, here an abuse or curse
Rishis and *Munis*	ancient sages
Ryot	peasant
Sahib	Sir
Sahib bahadur	head, chief, here Jail Superintendent
Salwar-kameez	baggy trousers and tunic
Sardar	Sikh
Sarkari	official, governmental
Satyagraha	non-violent resistance for truth
Sarvodaya	uplift of all

Sindhur	red powder used to mark forehead and for religious occasions
Tai	aunt
Takhti	wooden writing board
Tamasha	folk entertainment
Tau	uncle
Teena	tin
Tehsil	sub-division of a district
Tehsildar	collector of revenue in the tehsil
Thakur	upper caste landowner
Thali	metal plate used for eating food
Thana	police station
Thanadar	sub-inspector of police
Toli	group
Vedas	Hindu sacred books of period 2000—500 B.C.
Yuva Sabha	youth association
Zamindar	landlord
Zenana Khana	female ward

Abbreviations

ADM	Additional District Magistrate
AITUC	All-India Trades Union Congress (CPI-led)
ASI	Assistant Sub-Inspector of Police
ASP	Assistant Superintendent of Prisons
BLD	Bhartiya Lok Dal (Indian Peoples Party)
CPI	Communist Party of India
CPI (M)	Communist Party of India (Marxist)
CPI (M-L)	Communist Party of India (Marxist-Leninist)
DC	District Commissioner
DIR	Defence of India Rules
DSP	Deputy Superintendent of Police
DSP	Deputy Superintendent Prisons
IG	Inspector General of Police
IG (Prisons)	Inspector General (Prisons)
INTUC	Indian National Trade Union Congress (Congress-led)
MISA	Maintenance of Internal Security Act
MLC	Member Legislative Council
RSS	Rashtriya Swayam Sevak Sangh (National Volunteer Service Corps)
SHO	Station House Officer
SDM	Sub-Divisional Magistrate
SP	Superintendent of Police

Index

Akali Dal, support to Janata Party, 180

AITUC, Dehat Mazdoor Union affiliated to, 16, 91; Government partiality towards, 25

Allahabad High Court judgement against Mrs Gandhi, 12, 19, 24

Allende, Salvador, Mrs Gandhi's own comparison with, 24

Ambala jail ward, 104-106; corruption in, 107; prisoners' disunity in 107-108; prisoners' life in, 106-107

Ambala jail female ward, 19, 106-107; prisoners' background and profiles of, 108-113; struggle against a vindictive officer, 113-134, 140-145

Anand Marg, ban on, 24

Arjan Singh, Air Marshal, Mehrauli farm of, 35

Bank loans, bribery entailed in, 22

Bank nationalization and weaker sections, 22

Bansi Lal, as member of Mrs Gandhi's caucus, 113; defeat in 1977 elections, 180-181

Beg, Justice, as Supreme Court Chief Justice, 139

Bharat Ram, Mehrauli farm of, 33

B.L.D., 24; as Janata Party constituent, 180

Bhatia, General, Mehrauli farm of, 35

Birla, Mehrauli farm of, 33

Bombay Housewives' protest, 20

BBC, detenues' listening to, 105

Charat Ram, Mehrauli farm of, 33

Chawla, Navin, 79, 85; as ADM South Delhi, role of, 79-80; as special assistant to Lt-Governor, 94; malice of, 90

Coal nationalization, adverse impact of, 23

Compulsory Deposit Scheme and Workers' suppression, 26; see also Emergency

CPI, attitude to JP movement, 21; decimation in 1977 elections, 181; stance towards Mrs Gandhi, 15-16; support of Indira Government by, 26

CPI(M), attitude to JP movement, 21; stance towards Mrs Gandhi, 16; support to Janata Party, 180

CPI(M-L), attitude to JP movement 16; ban on, 24; detenu, 16

Congress(O), as Janata party constituent, 180

Congress, RSS-Jan Sangh view of, 99-101

Congress split of 1969, 22

Contract Labourers Act, 50

Dalmia, Mehrauli farm of, 33

De, Niren, on implications of emergency powers, 139

Dehat Mazdoor Sudhar Sabha, 50, 68; Dehat Mazdoor Union, 61, 81; affiliation to AITUC, 16, 91; affiliation to Khet Mazdoor Union, 91; executive members' detention under DIR, 31; formation of, 46; organization of, 61-63; registration of, 61; struggles of, 64-90; *see also* Mehrauli movement

Delhi Development Authority (DDA), rural land purchased and sold by, 32

Delhi Shops and Establishment Act, 66

Demolition Campaigns, 27

Desai, Morarji (Prime Minister), claim of, 182

DIR, emergency application of, 24

DMK, support to Janata Party, 180

Economic and Political Weekly, stance during Emergency, 25

Economic crisis, 21

Elections of 1977, 179; campaign of, 180; Indira Government's attitude during, 180; Janata Party's victory in, 180

Emergency declaration of, 5, 7, 24, 32, 94; and Bombay beggers, 27; and working of discipline, 26-28; and sterilization excess, 27-28; arrests measures immediately following, 24; big industry's pleasure at, 25; demolitions during, 27; farce of discipline during, 114; farce of resettlement, 26-27; Mrs Gandhi's explanation for, 24; Mrs Gandhi's motive behind, 19; revoked, 181; superficial improvements during, 28; trade union leaders' arrests during, 25; workers suppressed during, 25-26; *see* Gandhi, Mrs and Indira Gandhi Government

Emergency detenus, 15; communications network of, 105; harassment of, 164

Export incentives, impact on common man, 23

Factories Act, 50, 87

Farrer, Dean, human responses to society defined by, 1

Federation of Indian Chambers of Commerce and Industry (FICCI), approval of emergency by, 25

Female prisoners, 13-14; an insight into, 160, 162, 163, 170, 172; background and profiles of, 108-113, 115; inspired to protest, 120-122; love's triumph over, 170-172; *panchayat* experiment with, 156-160; quarrels among, 152, 154-155; protest of, 123-124, 131, 144-145

Gandhi, Mrs, 12, 20-23 79; Allahabad High court, judgement against, 19, 24; Bansi Lal's support to, 113; defeat in 1977 elections, 180-181; employers' false complaint to, 80; *Garibi Hatao* programme of, 31, 181; antagonism against author, 5; malice against author, 136; Mehrauli farm of, 33; 1977 elections announced by, 179-180; 20-point programme of, 24-28

Gandhi, Mahatma, assassination of, 98

Gandhi, Sanjay, 175; Bansi Lal's support to, 113; defeat in 1977 elections, 180-181; Navin Chawla's friendship with, 79

Garibi Hatao, Mrs Gandhi's slogan of, 31

Gujarat Student movement, 20

Habeaus corpus, Indira Government's plea to suspend, 135; suspension of, 135, 139
Har Dev Singh, author's lawyer, 137-138
Harijans, continued suppression of, 46-49
Hissar Borstal Institution and juvenile jail, author's transfer to, 148, 151; modernity of, 148, 151-152; *panchayat* experiment in, 156-160; prisoners' quarrels in, 152-155; *see also* jail administration

Indira Gandhi Government, authoritarian measures of, 23; emergency revoked by, 181; socialist measures of, 22-23
Indian Express, the, stance during emergency, 25
INTUC, Government partiality towards, 25
Indian Penal Code, section, 110
Industrial Disputes Act, 66

Jail administration, corruption and excess of, 106-107, 115-120, 124-134, 142-146; divide and rule practice of, 107, 140-141; job conditions in, 166-168; wasteful expenditure in, 168; *see also* Hissar Borstal institution and juvenile jail
Jaitly, Arun, as detenue, 16
Jamaat-e-Islami, ban on, 24; detenues, 16
Jana Sangh, and JP movement, 21; and RSS, 98; author's impression of, 98; common image of, 97-98; detenues, 16-19; ideology, practice and stance of, 98-101
Janata Government, author's assessment of, 181-182
Janata Party, formation of, 180; victory in 1977 elections, 180

JP movement, 19-21; author's asessment of, 20-21; political parties attitude to, 20-21; weakness of, 20
Job security, struggle for, 76
Judges, transfer and supercession of, 135

Kale, Pushpa, 141, 148, 149, 153, 158, 163, 167, 172. 174-175; as detenue, 139; in Ambala jail, 139; family background of, 166; personality of, 166; RSS release of, 179
Kapoor, V.K. as district Commissioner, role of, 79
Khanna, Justice, resignation from supreme Court, 139
Khet Mazdoor Union, Dehat Mazdoor Union's affiliation to, 91

Lajpat Rai, Lala, on measure of a country's prosperity, 181; open letter to Lloyd George, 181
Lee, Jennie, resettlement colonies dressed up to show, 27
Lewis, Charles (author's husband), 5, 9, 35, 146-147, 172-175; settlement in Delhi, 32
Lewis, Karoki (author's son), 5-10, 32, 102, 109, 146-147, 172-175; petition to Mrs Gandhi, 176; 10th birthday of, 183
Lewis, Primila (author), 80, 138-139; and Kamala Verma routine in Ambala jail, 103-105; arrival and settlement in Delhi, 32; attacked by farm owners' agent, 93; as detenu 17-19; bailed out, 90; Bombay experience of, 32; brief illness of, 165; case of detention, 138; conditions of parole, 175; detention under MISA, 6-11, 31; family reunion, 175-176; farewell from fellow prisoners, 174; first arrest of, 88; in Hissar jail, 151-167, 169-174; in Tihar

jail, 11-12; Mehrauli neigh-
bourhood of, 32-33, 35; Mrs
Gandhi's malice against, 136;
release on parole, 174, 176;
transfer to Hissar jail, 148;
transfer from Tihar jail, 15-16;
wild charges against, 58; wild
propaganda against, 71; writ
petition of, 134-135, 137-139;
writ petition statement of, 135,
186-192; *see also* Mahrauli
movement

Mehrauli movement, and police
apathy terrorization, 58, 63,
67, 69, 71, 78, 87, 88, 93-94;
benefit of workers' firmness,
68-70; cases of dismissed farm
workers, 56-59; case of farm
workers, 64-68; case of, workers'
exaggerated claims, 59-60; case
of workers' ration cards, 72-74;
case of police apathy, 58; confidence building programme of,
154-155; consolidation of, 74-75;
description of, 46-95; employers'
reaction, 70-71; factory workers
case, 81-90; first victory of, 56-
57; initial organization of, 52;
intellectuals' participation in,
53; lessons of a defeat, 68;
medical scheme of, 53; struggle
for legal minimum wage, 76-
79; union organization by, 61-
63; *see also* Dehat Mazdoor
Union
Malaviya, K.D., Mehrauli farm of,
33
Malhotra, Vijay Kumar, under
detention, 16, 18
MISA, 135, 151; emergency application of, 24; misuse of, 13
MISA detenues, 114; defence of
138; rules for, 105; *see also*
Emergency detenues
MISA regulations, flouting of, 153
McNamara, Robert, approval of
Mrs Gandhi's sterilization cam-

paigns, 26, 169-170
Minimum Wages Act, 50, 61; continued tardy implementation
of, 183; employers' flouting of,
78; provisions of, 55-56; struggle for implementation of,
76-79
Minorities and Scheduled Castes,
congress exploitation of, 100-
101
Muslim Majlis, ban on, 24; detenues
16
Muzaffarnagar firing, 27-28

Narain, Raj, 24; detention of, 12
Narayan, Jayaprakash, blessings to
Janata Party, 180
National Integration, RSS-Jan
Sangh view on, 99-100
Nayar, Kuldip, release from deten-
tion, 134
Naxalites, attitude to JP movement,
21; ban on, 24; RSS assess-
ment of, 18; tortures inflicted
on, 17
Nehru, B.K., Mehrauli farm of, 33

Paolo Freire, 53
Phool Kumari Singh, Mrs, (Jail
officer) relation with Bansi
Lal, 113; vindictive role of,
113-134, 140-145
Police, complaint of, 136
Police apathy, terrorization, 58, 63,
67-69, 71, 78, 87-88, 93-94
Police excesses, 109, 111-113
Political crisis, 21, 23
Poverty line, people below, 21
Press censorship, emergency impo-
sition of, 24
Preventive detention laws, emer-
gency application of, 24
Privy Purse abolition, farce of, 22

Radio Pakistan, emergency detenues' listening to, 105
Railway strike of 1974, ruthless
suppression of, 23

Rajmata of Jodhpur, Mehrauli farm of, 35

Ram, Jagjivan, sudden defection of, 180

RSS, and Gandhi's assassination, 98, and Jana Sangh, 98; assessment of Naxalites by, 18; ban on, 24; common image of, 98; detenues, 16-18; ideology practice and stance of, 98-102

Rathi, Dharam Singh, as detenue, 148; view on emergency repercussions, 149; Bansi Lal's malice against, 150; personality of, 150

Rawley, Genera, Mehrauli farm of, 35

Resettlement scheme, farce of, 26-27

Schwarz, Walter, interest in Mehrauli movement, 80

Singh, Satya Narain (CPI-ML), attitude to JP movement, 21; *see also* Naxalites

Sinha, Justice, 24

Social Work, current practice of, 53

Socialist Party, and JP movement, 21; as Janata Party constituent, 180; detenues, 16

Soviet Union, support of Indira Government by, 26

Srilata, 14, 76, 93-94, 135-136, 138, 146, 182; case of detention, 138; detention under MISA, 9-10, 31; in Tihar jail, 11-12; meeting author in jail, 12; release on parole, 147

Sterilization campaigns, excesses of, 27-28, 169-170

Supreme Court, ruling on Habeas corpus suspension, 139

Tata, Mehrauli farm of, 33

Thatcher, Margret, resettlement colonies dressed up to show, 27

Thoreau, on civil disobedience, 3

Tihar jail, 11-14, 135; female ward of, 106; female prisoners of, 13-14; lifers' jail break from 139; overstuffin of, 139; political detenues in, 18

Total Revolution, 20; *see also* JP movement

Tripathi, Laxman, *Barrack Chayya*, 3, 103

Trade Union Act, 50-51

Trade Unionism, corruption in, 53

Turkman Gate demolitions, 27

20-point programme, farce of, 24-28, 31-32, 150, 181-182; *see also* Gandhi, Mrs

Verma, Dr Kamla, 97, 139, 141, 148 152-153, 158, 167; illness of, 163; on RSS-Jan Sangh ideology and stance, 98-101; personality of, 101-102; release of, 179; retransfer to Ambala jail, 126; transfer to Karnal jail, 102; transfer to Rohtak, 164; under detention, 19

"Weaker sections" of population, 36-46; Mrs Gandhi's socialism and, 22-23

Workman's compensation Act, 50, 66

Yunus, Mohammed, 138